Irish Cooking

Acknowledgments

The writing and preparation of an illustrated book such as this involves a considerable number of people and an enormous amount of effort and dedication. I am indebted to all those who made it possible, particularly Edwin Higel of Brookside Publishing Services who introduced me to Hamlyn and without whose encouragement and support it might never have happened. To Susan Haynes who commissioned the book and, in fact, did make it happen and who has enthused about it since its inception. To Sasha Judelson, my editor, who made sure everything was just right and to the designer Mette Heinz, who has worked the materials into a most attractive package.

One of the most important features of such a book is undoubtedly the photographs. Once again I am indebted to my friend Christopher Hill, whose wonderful lighting and sensitivity not only brought the food, dishes and settings to life, but provided the perfect atmosphere in which to work.

In the studio I was assisted by Ann Macfarlane with whom I have worked for the past twenty years and whose meticulous perfectionism and support I have relied on during every project. Without her help, wise council and friendship, such an exercise would have been incomplete and much less enjoyable. Peggy Hanna has also contributed greatly in all my books, assisting Ann and myself, and making sure that we were never short of cups of tea and coffee. I also wish to thank Christopher Hill's assistants, in particular John MacAfee and his long-suffering secretary Janet Smith.

I would like to thank the Ulster Folk and Transport Museum and in particular Fionnuala Carragher, Assistant Keeper (Domestic Life), for supplying many of the artifacts used in the photographs. In addition, I wish to thank Robert Huffam, antique dealer and collector, for an unending supply of culinary memorabilia from his props warehouse; and Albert Forsythe, antique dealer, and his wife Margaret, for many pieces from their collection.

Last but not least I must thank Alison Gray who, with the wonders of modern technology, turned my manuscript into a perfectly presented document.

First published in Great Britain in 1996 by
Hamlyn a division of Octopus Publishing Group Ltd

This edition published in 2012 by Bounty Books,
a division of Octopus Publishing Group Ltd
Endeavour House
189 Shaftesbury Avenue
London WC2H 8JY
www.octopusbooks.co.uk

An Hachette UK Company
www.hachette.co.uk

Reprinted 2004, 2006, 2007, 2008, 2009, 2010

ISBN: 978-0-753723-24-1

A CIP catalogue record for this book is available from the British Library

Printed and bound in China

IRISH COOKING

OVER 100 TRADITIONAL IRISH RECIPES

page 67 Irish Stew.

CLARE CONNERY

Both metric and imperial measurements have been given in all recipes.
Use one set of measurements only and not a mixture of both.

Standard level spoon measurements are used in all recipes.
1 tablespoon = one 15 ml spoon
1 teaspoon = one 5 ml spoon

Eggs should be medium unless otherwise stated.

Milk should be full fat unless otherwise stated.

Pepper should be freshly ground.

Fresh herbs should be used unless otherwise stated. If unavailable, use dried herbs as an alternative but halve the given quantities.

Ovens should be preheated to the specified temperature – if using a fan assisted oven, follow the manufacturer's instructions for adjusting the time and temperature.

To test if poultry is cooked, pierce the flesh through the thickest part with a skewer or fork – the juices should run clear, never pink or red.

Introduction

I write this looking out from my cottage window overlooking Strangford Lough in Co Down, where the relentless ebb and flow of the tide seems to evoke the awesome power of nature and epitomize how much we in Ireland have suffered from its vagaries, as well as relied upon and benefited from its bounty. This bounty I first experienced as a child, when I sat by the hearth in my Grandmother's farmhouse kitchen and watched her produce wholesome stews, rich roasts, puddings, cakes and a vast variety of bread over a turf fire. Indeed, I can still recall the wonderful aromas to this day. I helped her milk cows, feed chickens, turkeys and ducks, pick potatoes, plant vegetables and gather wild berries from the mountain and bog land. Food was always fresh, plentiful and tasty, the quality superb and the variety, in those days, enormous. The dishes may not have been sophisticated but they were sustaining and delicious.

Over the years I have added to these experiences by talking to people all over Ireland, by watching them cook and through cooking myself, both for family and friends as well as commercially. In recent years I have devoted much time to researching the history of Irish food, in order to understand and appreciate the core values of Irish culture, in which food plays such a vital part. This has enabled me not only to recreate recipes which embody the best from Ireland's culinary heritage and its vast wealth of natural resources, but to combine them with modern methods, techniques and culinary influences from other parts of the world in order to illustrate the style of Irish cooking which is evolving today. This book is a celebration of all these traditions from past to present, and a tribute to the people of a country where the quality of life is among the finest in Europe.

Dedication: for Bruce

The ever-bubbling pot of soup has been the central theme in the Irish diet: in times of poverty as the mainstay of the people; in times of plenty it is warm and comforting.

Soup can be made from whatever ingredients are available, to provide everything from an appetizing first course to a dish so substantial and sustaining that it is a meal in itself.

Soups

Cream of Watercress Soup

Wash the watercress well, discarding any damaged or yellow leaves. Reserve 6 small sprigs for garnishing and roughly chop the remainder. Melt the butter in a large saucepan. Stir in the watercress, leek, onion and potatoes, cover closely with a piece of greaseproof paper and sweat over a very gentle heat for about 20 minutes without colouring.

Add the stock or water, bring to the boil, then reduce the heat and simmer for 10–15 minutes, until the vegetables are tender.

Purée the soup in a liquidizer or food processor until smooth. Return to the saucepan, stir in the cream and season to taste with salt, pepper and nutmeg. Bring to the boil and serve immediately in individual soup bowls. Garnish each bowl with a sprig of the reserved watercress.

Cook's Tip
To 'sweat' in cooking terms means to draw out the juices and flavour from food, generally vegetables. This is done by first softening them in a little butter or oil, then covering them closely with greaseproof paper to keep the steam in and cooking over a very low heat until the vegetables are beginning to soften; they should not colour. This process will usually take about 15–30 minutes.

Preparation time
15 minutes

Cooking time
30–35 minutes

Serves 4–6

You will need
150 g/5 oz watercress
25 g/1 oz butter
1 large leek, white part only, sliced
1 large onion, chopped
2 potatoes, chopped
1 litre/1¾ pints chicken stock or water
150 ml/¼ pint single cream
salt and pepper
pinch of ground nutmeg

Carrot and Herb Soup

Melt the butter in a large saucepan, add the onion, garlic, carrots and potato and cook gently over a low heat until soft but not coloured. Add the stock, bouquet garni, mace, salt and pepper. Bring to the boil, then reduce the heat and simmer gently for 45 minutes–1 hour, until the vegetables are tender.

Remove the bouquet garni and purée the soup in a liquidizer or food processor until smooth. Return to the saucepan, add the cream and bring to the boil. Mix the herbs together and stir three-quarters of them into the soup. Serve in individual soup bowls, garnished with the croûtons and remaining herbs.

Cook's Tips
A bouquet garni is a bunch of fresh herbs tied together with kitchen string. It generally consists of parsley stalks, a sprig of thyme and a bay leaf. Optional additions include a blade of mace, a piece of celery stick or a piece of leek. It is added to soups and stews to give additional flavour.

To make croûtons, remove the crusts from 2 slices of bread and cut each slice into 5 mm/1/4 inch cubes. Fry in a little hot oil, stirring frequently, until golden brown on all sides. Drain on absorbent kitchen paper before use.

Preparation time
10 minutes

Cooking time
1 hour

Serves 6

You will need
25 g/1 oz butter
1 large onion, finely sliced
1 garlic clove, chopped
500 g/1 lb carrots, sliced
1 small potato, sliced
1 litre/1¾ pints chicken stock
bouquet garni (Cook's Tip)
pinch of ground mace
150 ml/¼ pint single cream
2 tablespoons finely chopped coriander
1 tablespoon finely chopped parsley
1 tablespoon finely chopped chervil
salt and pepper
croûtons, to garnish (Cook's Tip)

Potato Soup with Bacon and Chives

Melt the butter in a large saucepan and fry the onion until soft, without colouring. Add the potatoes, stock and milk, and season with salt and pepper. Bring to the boil, then reduce the heat and simmer for 40–45 minutes, stirring occasionally to prevent the potatoes from sticking.

Purée the soup in a liquidizer or food processor until smooth. Return to the saucepan, taste and adjust the seasoning and stir in the cream and bacon. Bring to the boil and serve in individual soup bowls, garnished with snipped chives.

Cook's Tip
Vegetable stock can be used instead of the chicken stock, if preferred.

Preparation time
15–20 minutes

Cooking time
45–50 minutes

Serves 6–8

You will need
50 g/2 oz butter
1 large onion, roughly chopped
750 g/1½ lb potatoes, peeled and roughly chopped
750 ml/1¼ pints chicken stock
750 ml/1¼ pints milk
50 ml/2 fl oz single cream
6 rashers of streaky bacon, chopped and fried until crisp
salt and pepper
1 tablespoon snipped chives, to garnish

Celeriac and Blue Cheese Soup

Melt the butter in a large saucepan and fry the onions and celeriac over a gentle heat for a few minutes. Add the stock, bring to the boil, then simmer over a low heat for 30 minutes, until the celeriac is tender.

Purée the soup in a liquidizer or food processor until smooth. Return to the saucepan, add the cream and bring to the boil. Reduce the heat, add the cheese and stir until melted. Taste and season with salt and pepper if necessary. Serve in individual soup bowls, garnished with croûtons and snipped chives.

Cook's Tips
One of Ireland's most famous and delicious cheeses is rich, creamy Cashel Blue. It is the perfect cheese for this soup, although any blue cheese can be used.

If celeriac is difficult to obtain, celery can be used instead.

Preparation time
15 minutes

Cooking time
40 minutes

Serves 6–7

You will need
25 g/1 oz butter
2 onions, chopped
875 g/13⁄4 lb celeriac, to give about 425 g/14 oz when peeled and roughly chopped
1 litre/13⁄4 pints chicken stock
150 ml/1⁄4 pint single cream
125 g/4 oz blue cheese, ideally Cashel Blue, rind removed and cut into pieces
salt and pepper

To garnish
croûtons (Cook's Tip, page 10)
1 tablespoon snipped chives

Sorrel Soup

Melt the butter in a large saucepan, add the onion and potatoes and cook gently for about 1 minute. Add the chicken stock, bring to the boil and simmer gently for 25–30 minutes, until the vegetables are tender.

Add the sorrel leaves and cook for a further 5 minutes. Purée the soup in a liquidizer or food processor until smooth. Return to the saucepan, add the cream and season to taste with salt and pepper. Bring to the boil and serve in individual soup bowls, garnished with chervil.

Cook's Tip
If fresh sorrel is difficult to obtain, replace with watercress or spinach. Wash well and discard any discoloured leaves and coarse stems.

Preparation time
15 minutes

Cooking time
30–35 minutes

Serves 4

You will need
50 g/2 oz butter
1 onion, chopped
500 g/1 lb potatoes, roughly diced
900 ml/1½ pints chicken stock
250 g/8 oz sorrel, shredded, large stems removed
150 ml/¼ pint double cream
salt and pepper
fresh chervil leaves, to garnish

Mussel Soup with Saffron and Garlic

Prepare the mussels (Cook's Tip). Put 25 g/1 oz of the butter in a very large saucepan, add one-third of the onion and leek and cook until soft. Add the mussels, 1 bouquet garni and the white wine. Cover the pan and cook over a high heat for 4–5 minutes, stirring the mussels from time to time.

When the mussel shells have opened, drain through a muslin-lined sieve set over a bowl to catch the cooking juices. Remove the mussels from their shells, discarding any mussels which did not open. Refrigerate until required.

Gently fry the remaining vegetables and garlic in the rest of the butter until soft. Add the fish stock and reserved mussel cooking juices and the remaining bouquet garni. Add the mussels, reserving 12 to garnish the soup. Bring to the boil and cook gently for 20 minutes.

Remove the bouquet garni, add the saffron and cream and purée in a liquidizer or food processor until smooth. Return to the pan, taste and adjust the seasoning if necessary. Stir in the reserved whole mussels. Bring to the boil and serve immediately in individual soup bowls, garnished with chervil.

Cook's Tip

To prepare mussels, wash under cold running water and scrape, removing the beard (the hairy attachment protruding from the mussel) and any barnacles attached to the shells. Discard any mussels that are open or damaged.

Preparation time
30 minutes

Cooking time
25 minutes

Serves 4–6

You will need

about 1.5 kg/3 lb fresh, live mussels
75 g/3 oz butter
1 onion, finely sliced
175 g/6 oz leek, white part only, finely sliced
2 bouquets garnis (see page 10)
125 ml/4 fl oz dry white wine
175 g/6 oz carrot, finely sliced
1 celery stick, finely sliced
72 garlic cloves, crushed
50 ml/1¼ pints fish stock (see page 45)
pinch of saffron threads
150 ml/¼ pint double cream
salt and pepper
fresh chervil leaves, to garnish

Lentil and Ham Broth

Rinse the ham shank in cold water then put it into a large saucepan and cover with cold water. Bring to the boil. This will remove any excess salt from the ham and bring any scum to the surface. Drain off the water, rinse the pan and start again with 2.5 litres/4 pints fresh cold water. Add the lentils, onions, carrots and turnip, bring to the boil, then reduce the heat and simmer for 1½ hours.

Add the potatoes and cook for a further 30 minutes, until the meat is tender and the broth rich and thick. Remove the ham from the broth, peel off the skin and cut the meat into small cubes. Add the ham cubes to the broth, season to taste with salt and pepper and stir in the parsley. Serve hot.

Cook's Tip
The cooked ham shank also makes an excellent main course dish. Remove the skin, press toasted breadcrumbs and brown sugar into the fat and stud with whole cloves. Roast in a preheated oven at 220°C (425°F), Gas Mark 7, in a little hot fat for 15–30 minutes, until crisp and brown.

Preparation time
15 minutes

Cooking time
2 hours

Serves 8–10

You will need
1 ham shank
(500 g–1 kg/1–2 lb in weight)
175 g/6 oz split red lentils, rinsed
2 large onions, finely diced
2 large carrots (about 500 g/1 lb), finely diced
175 g/6 oz turnip, finely diced
500 g/1 lb potatoes, finely diced
3 tablespoons finely chopped parsley
salt and pepper

White Onion Soup with Soda Bread Croûtons

Melt the butter in a large saucepan. Add the onions and leek. Cover closely with a piece of greaseproof paper and the lid and cook very gently without colouring, stirring frequently, for about 30 minutes.

Sprinkle the flour over the onions and stir well to blend. Gradually add the water or chicken stock. Bring to the boil, then reduce the heat and simmer for 15 minutes.

While the soup is cooking prepare the croûtons by cutting the soda farl into 5 mm/¼ inch cubes and frying in hot oil in a large frying pan until an even golden colour. Remove from the pan using a slotted spoon and drain on absorbent kitchen paper.

Taste and season the soup with salt and pepper, add the cream and return to the boil. Serve in individual soup bowls, with a sprinkling of croûtons on top.

Cook's Tip
For an attractive presentation a little of the cream can be reserved and swirled on top of the soup just before serving. For an entirely different texture the soup can be puréed in a liquidizer or food processor before adding the cream.

Preparation time
15 minutes

Cooking time
about 45 minutes

Serves 4–6

You will need
50 g/2 oz butter
500 g/1 lb white onions, very thinly sliced
1 leek, white part only (about 50 g/2 oz), thinly sliced
40 g/1½ oz plain flour
1 litre/1¾ pints water or chicken stock
½ Soda Farl (see page 120)
oil, for shallow frying
salt and white pepper
150 ml/¼ pint single cream

Leek and Potato Soup

Melt the butter in a large saucepan, add the leeks, potatoes and onion. Stir well to coat with the butter. Cover closely with a piece of greaseproof paper and cook over a very gentle heat for about 15 minutes until softened, stirring frequently to prevent the vegetables from colouring.

Add the stock or water and the milk, bring to the boil, then reduce the heat and simmer gently for about 20 minutes, until the vegetables are tender.

Purée the soup in a liquidizer or food processor until smooth. Return to the saucepan, taste and season with salt and pepper and when very hot pour into individual bowls and serve, garnished with chives.

Cook's Tip
In the summer this soup can be served very cold to make a most refreshing first course. A little more stock will be needed to thin the consistency slightly.

Preparation time
15 minutes

Cooking time
35 minutes

Serves 4–6

You will need
25 g/1 oz butter
2 large leeks, finely sliced
250 g/8 oz potatoes, roughly diced
1 onion, roughly chopped
750 ml/1¼ pints chicken stock or water
300 ml/½ pint milk
salt and pepper
1 tablespoon snipped chives, to garnish

Celery and Lovage Soup with Herb Cream and Croûtons

Melt the butter in a large saucepan. Add the celery, onion, leek and potatoes and sweat over a gentle heat for about 15 minutes, until soft but not coloured. Stir in the lovage leaves and pour over the stock and milk. Season with salt and pepper, bring to the boil, then reduce the heat and simmer for about 20–25 minutes.

Purée the soup in a liquidizer or food processor until smooth. Return to the saucepan, taste and adjust the seasoning and consistency, if necessary. Bring the soup to the boil.

Mix the cream with the chopped herbs, reserving a few for the garnish. Pour the hot soup into 4 soup bowls, spoon a little herb cream on top of each bowl, and sprinkle with the reserved herbs, the celery seeds and croûtons. Serve at once.

Cook's Tip
Lovage is a herb with a flavour somewhat similar to celery; if it is difficult to obtain, celery leaves can be substituted.

Preparation time
15 minutes

Cooking time
40–45 minutes

Serves 4

50 g/2 oz butter
375 g/12 oz trimmed celery sticks, chopped
1 onion, chopped
1 small leek, white part only, sliced
125 g/4 oz potatoes, cubed
3 lovage leaves, chopped
600 ml/1 pint chicken stock
300 ml/½ pint milk
150 ml/¼ pint double cream, lightly whipped
3 tablespoons parsley, chives and lovage, finely chopped
salt and pepper

To garnish
¼ teaspoon celery seeds
croûtons (Cook's Tip, page10)

Spinach and Oatmeal Broth

Melt the butter in a large saucepan and fry the onion until soft but not coloured. Stir in the oatmeal and continue to cook until the oatmeal is beginning to colour slightly.

Wash the spinach, remove and discard any tough stalks and chop the leaves roughly. Add to the pan along with the potatoes, stock, a pinch of nutmeg, salt and pepper. Bring to the boil, then reduce the heat and simmer gently for about 10–20 minutes or until the spinach is just cooked.

Purée the soup in a liquidizer or food processor until smooth. Return to the pan, add the milk or cream, taste and adjust the seasoning if necessary. Bring to the boil and serve immediately in individual soup bowls. Sprinkle each bowl with a little nutmeg and oatmeal.

Cook's Tips
This soup can be made with sorrel instead of spinach, or a mixture of both.

Cook the spinach for the minimum amount of time, in order to retain its bright green colour.

Preparation time
5 minutes

Cooking time
40 minutes

Serves 4–6

You will need
50 g/2 oz butter
1 onion, chopped
20 g/¾ oz rolled oats or fine oatmeal, plus extra, to garnish
275 g/9 oz spinach
50 g/2 oz potatoes, diced
750 ml/1¼ pints chicken stock
ground nutmeg
65 ml/2½ fl oz milk or single cream
salt and pepper

Game Broth with Potato and Herb Dumplings

Put all the ingredients for the soup into a large saucepan, bring to the boil, reduce the heat and simmer for 20 minutes, until the vegetables are tender.

Meanwhile, prepare the dumplings. Melt the butter in a saucepan, add the onion and cook gently until soft; do not allow it to colour. Stir into the mashed potatoes along with the semolina, parsley, thyme and nutmeg. Add a little beaten egg and enough flour to make a stiff mixture. Roll teaspoons of the mixture into 16 balls, using a little flour to prevent the mixture from sticking. Drop the dumplings into the hot soup and simmer for 10 minutes, until they float to the surface. Divide the dumplings between 8 soup bowls and ladle the broth over them. Garnish with sprigs of parsley and serve immediately.

Cook's Tip
This is an excellent way of using leftover bones and trimmings from roast game. To make the stock, brown 750 g/1½ lb game bones in a little oil with 1 large carrot, 1 large onion, 1 large leek and 1 celery stick, all roughly sliced. Add 2.5 litres/4 pints water and a bunch of fresh herbs. Bring to the boil, then simmer gently for at least 2 hours. Strain and reduce to 1.7 litres/2¾ pints.

Preparation time
20 minutes

Cooking time
30 minutes

Serves 8

You will need
1.7 litres/2¾ pints game stock (Cook's Tip)
1 onion, finely diced
1 carrot, finely diced
1 celery stick , finely diced
125 g/4 oz turnip, finely diced
1 large potato, finely diced
sprigs of parsley, to garnish

Dumplings
15 g/½ oz butter
1 tablespoon finely chopped onion
250 g/8 oz potatoes, cooked and mashed
1 tablespoon semolina
2 tablespoons finely chopped parsley
pinch of chopped freshly thyme
pinch of ground nutmeg
beaten egg, to bind
2 tablespoons plain flour
salt and pepper

Ham and Pea Soup

Melt the butter in a large saucepan and fry the onion, carrot and two-thirds of the bacon over a gentle heat until soft; this will take about 15 minutes. Add the drained peas, bay leaf, ham bone and water or stock. Bring to the boil, then reduce the heat and simmer gently for 1 hour.

Discard the ham bone and bay leaf. Taste and season the soup with black pepper and salt if necessary. Fry the remaining bacon in a hot pan until crisp, then add to the soup along with 1 tablespoon of the chives. Serve in individual soup bowls and garnish with the remaining chives.

Cook's Tips
Whole dried peas can be used to make this soup but will need cooking for an extra hour.

If the soup is made with ham stock instead of water, the ham bone can be omitted.

Preparation time
10 minutes, plus soaking time

Cooking time
1¼ hours

Serves 6

You will need
50 g/2 oz butter
1 large onion, roughly chopped
1 large carrot, roughly chopped
4 thick rashers of bacon (about 175 g/6 oz), rinded, and diced
250 g/8 oz yellow or green split peas (soaked for 4–6 hours)
1 small bay leaf
1 ham bone
1.2 litres/2 pints water or ham stock
2 tablespoons finely chopped chives
salt and black pepper

The wide variety of fine natural ingredients has inspired the Irish cook to create a range of first-course dishes as an alternative to the traditional soup. Ranging from rustic pâtés to a delicate salmon mousse, these dishes can also be served as light lunches or suppers.

Starters and Snacks

Chicken Liver Pâté with Spiced Apples

Fry the onion and garlic in half the butter until soft, add the chicken livers with the remaining butter and continue to fry over a gentle heat until cooked and beginning to brown slightly; this will take about 15–20 minutes.

Turn up the heat, add the brandy, parsley and seasoning and cook quickly for a few minutes. Leave to cool slightly, then blend in a liquidizer or food processor until very smooth. Pack into 4 small (50 ml/2 fl oz) moulds, cover each with a thin layer of clarified butter, then leave until the butter has set firm and the pâtés are completely cold.

To make the spiced apples, put the sugar, vinegar and spices into a saucepan over a gentle heat, bring to the boil and simmer for 3–4 minutes. Add the sliced apples and simmer for a further 3–4 minutes, until just tender. Leave the apples in the syrup until they are completely cold.

Serve the pâté in the moulds or turn out on to 4 serving plates. Garnish with salad leaves and serve with spiced apples and warm toast.

Preparation time
10–15 minutes

Cooking time
15–20 minutes

Serves 4

You will need
1 onion, finely chopped
2 garlic cloves, crushed
50 g/2 oz butter
250 g/8 oz chicken livers, trimmed and roughly chopped if large
2 teaspoons brandy
1 tablespoon finely chopped parsley
clarified butter (Cook's Tip, page 53)
salt and pepper

Spiced apples
250 g/8 oz sugar
300 ml/½ pint cider vinegar
8 cloves
2.5 cm/1 inch cinnamon stick
¼ teaspoon allspice berries
4 apples (preferably Cox's Pippins), peeled, cored and roughly sliced

To serve
salad leaves
white or brown Soda Bread (see pages 114–115), toasted

Pork and Bacon Terrine with Honey Pickled Vegetables

Brush a 1.2 litre/2 pint terrine mould with a little oil and line with overlapping rashers of bacon, allowing 5 cm/2 inches to fall over the terrine edge. Mix together the onions, parsley and pepper. Slice the pork fillets lengthways so that they can be opened out into one flat piece. Flatten each one, just enough to fit into the terrine, and trim to size. Lay one fillet in the bottom of the terrine, spread half of the onion and parsley mixture on top, then repeat, finishing with pork fillet. Fold the overhanging bacon on top of the pork, pour on the white wine and arrange the bay leaves on top. Cover with foil and place in a roasting dish with enough hot water to come three-quarters of the way up the terrine. Place in a preheated oven at 160°C (325°F), Gas Mark 3 for 1½ hours, or until cooked through.

Leave to cool, then weigh down and leave to set in the refrigerator overnight. Slice and serve with honey pickled vegetables and a few salad leaves.

Cook's Tip
To check that the terrine is cooked, insert a fine skewer into the centre and leave for 30 seconds. Remove and test with care: if the skewer is too hot to hold against the bottom lip or the back of the hand, then the terrine is cooked.

Preparation time
30 minutes

Cooking time
1½ hours

Oven temperature
160°C (325°F), Gas Mark 3

Serves 12

You will need
vegetable oil
12–14 rashers of unsmoked back bacon
2 large onions, finely chopped
25 g/1 oz finely chopped fresh parsley
1 tablespoon white pepper
3 pork fillets, about 375 g/12 oz each
150 ml/¼ pint dry white wine
3 bay leaves

To serve
Honey Pickled Vegetables (see page 93)
salad leaves

Hot Salmon Mousse with Hollandaise Sauce

Cut the salmon into pieces and blend in a food processor until smooth. With the machine running, add the egg whites followed by the cream in a steady stream. Stir in the chopped dill and season with salt and pepper.

Brush 6 x 100 ml/3½ fl oz dariole moulds or ramekin dishes with the oil and line with clingfilm. Divide the mousse mixture between the moulds, levelling the top with the back of a lightly oiled spoon. Place in a roasting dish filled with enough warm water to come three-quarters of the way up the sides of the moulds. Place in a preheated oven at 150°C (300°F) ,Gas Mark 2 for 15–20 minutes, until the mousse has set.

While the mousse is cooking prepare the hollandaise sauce. Put the egg yolks and white wine vinegar into the bowl of a food processor. Blend to combine. With the machine running, gradually pour in the warm clarified butter. Process until all the butter has been added and the sauce is thick. Blend in 2 tablespoons hot water and serve immediately.

To serve, unmould each mousse on to the centre of a hot serving plate, spoon on a little sauce and garnish with a sprig of chervil or dill. Serve immediately.

Preparation time
20 minutes

Cooking time
15–20 minutes

Oven temperature
150°C (300°F), Gas Mark 2

Serves 6

You will need
425 g/14 oz fresh salmon, skinned and boned
2 egg whites
250 ml/8 fl oz single cream
½ teaspoon finely chopped dill
1 tablespoon vegetable oil
salt and pepper
6 sprigs of chervil or dill, to garnish

Hollandaise sauce
3 egg yolks
1 tablespoon white wine vinegar
175 ml/6 fl oz warm clarified butter (Cook's Tip, page 53)
2 tablespoons hot water

Irish Smoked Salmon with Wheaten Bread

The best way to eat wonderful Irish smoked salmon is simply cut in generous slices and served with fine wheaten bread.

Milled black pepper, finely chopped onion and capers are the traditional 'hotel' garnish, but I believe the delicate taste of the fish should not be overpowered by such additions. The only garnish needed is a wedge of lemon.

Cook's Tips
Good quality smoked salmon should be moist and delicate in colour. It can be bought ready-sliced in packs, or as whole sides, sliced or unsliced, from delicatessens and fishmongers. When presliced it is generally cut thinly; when cutting it yourself you can allow more generous slices.

To make a quick smoked salmon pâté, mix equal quantities of smoked salmon pieces or trimmings and curd or soft cheese in a food processor with lemon juice and black pepper to taste. Allow 50 g/2 oz salmon and cheese per person.

Preparation time
5 minutes

Serves 4

You will need
250–300 g/8–10 oz Irish smoked salmon, sliced
Irish Wheaten Bread (see page 115), sliced and buttered
1 lemon, cut into 4 wedges

Black Pudding with Apple Purée and Leeks

Put the apples and water in a saucepan, cover and cook over a very gentle heat until soft and pulpy, stirring frequently to prevent burning. Stir in the sugar and sage, and season to taste with pepper. Beat with a wooden spoon to give a textured purée. Keep warm.

Steam or boil the leeks until tender; drain well. Melt the butter in a large frying pan and fry the black pudding for a few minutes on each side, until very hot.

Spoon a mound of apple purée in the centre of 4 hot serving plates and arrange 3–4 slices of black pudding on top. Scatter the leeks around the edge of the apple and black pudding and serve immediately, garnished with sprigs of chervil and sage.

Cook's Tips

The best black puddings in Ireland come from West Cork and have the delicate texture of an egg custard. My favourite is 'Clonakilty' made by Edward Twomey.

Traditionally, black pudding is fried in bacon fat and served as part of an Irish Fry (see page 64).

Preparation time
10–15 minutes

Cooking time
10 minutes

Serves 4

You will need

1 kg/2 lb Bramley apples, peeled, cored and sliced
1 tablespoon water
1 tablespoon sugar
1 sage leaf, finely chopped
175 g/6 oz white part of leek, cut into fine 5 cm/2 inch lengths
50 g/2 oz butter
250–300 g/8–10 oz black pudding, cut into 12–16 slices
black pepper
sprigs of chervil and sage, to garnish

CLONAKILTY
CLONAKILTY
CLONAKILTY

Irish Smoked Salmon with Potato Cakes, Soured Cream and Chives

Prepare the potato cakes by putting all the ingredients into a bowl and mixing gently with a wooden spoon to form a light dough. Turn on to a lightly floured work surface and roll out to about 1 cm/½ inch thick. Cut into 4 circles, using a 5 cm/ 2½ inch plain cutter.

Warm a heavy frying pan over a gentle heat until a light dusting of flour just begins to turn a very pale fawn colour. Keep the pan at this temperature and add the potato cakes. Cook for a few minutes until lightly browned on each side.

While the potato cakes are cooking, divide the smoked salmon between 4 serving plates, arranging it on one side. Allow the potato cakes to cool slightly then place one on each plate beside the salmon. Arrange the diced tomatoes on top of the potato cakes, then top each potato cake with soured cream and garnish with chives. Serve immediately.

Cook's Tip
These potato cakes are equally good served with bacon and eggs as part of an Irish Fry (see page 64) or alternatively just eat them hot with butter and homemade jam.

Preparation time
10 minutes

Cooking time
8 minutes

Serves 4

You will need
250 g/8 oz potatoes, cooked
25 g/1 oz butter, melted
50 g/2 oz plain flour, plus extra for shaping and cooking
pinch of salt

To serve
250–300 g/8–10 oz smoked salmon, thinly sliced
4 tablespoons thick soured cream
2 tomatoes, deseeded and diced
snipped chives, to garnish

Pan-Fried Dublin Bay Prawn Tails with Herbs

Heat the butter in a large frying pan, add the garlic and fry over a gentle heat until soft but not coloured. Stir in half the herbs, increase the heat, add the prawns and cover with a lid. Cook for about 3 minutes, shaking the pan frequently to toss the prawns and ensure even cooking. Taste and season with salt and pepper.

Remove the prawns from the pan and divide between 2 warmed serving plates, arranging the prawns flesh side up. Add the remaining chopped herbs to the juices in the pan, stir to mix, then pour over the prawns. Serve immediately, garnished with a lemon wedge, a sprig of watercress and a few sprigs of herbs.

Cook's Tip

Dublin Bay prawns are not prawns at all but members of the lobster family, hence their Latin name *Nephrops norvegicus* (Norwegian lobster); they are also known as langoustines or scampi. They are a great delicacy and one of the most highly prized and highly priced shellfish caught off the Irish coast. Like all shellfish they should be very fresh or frozen and bought from a good fishmonger.

Preparation time
5 minutes

Cooking time
3–4 minutes

Serves 2

You will need

125 g/4 oz clarified butter (Cook's Tip, page 53)
1 garlic clove, crushed
4 tablespoons mixed herbs, e.g. parsley, tarragon and chervil, very finely chopped
12 fresh Dublin Bay prawn tails, in their shells, washed and split in half lengthways, with the gut removed
salt and pepper

To garnish

½ lemon, cut into 2 wedges
sprigs of watercress
sprigs of fresh herbs

Irish Smoked Salmon with Scrambled Eggs

Break the eggs into a small bowl and mix well with a fork, but do not beat. Stir in the milk and season with salt and pepper. Melt the butter in a saucepan until it begins to foam. Pour in the egg mixture and cook over a gentle heat, stirring constantly with a wooden spoon, scraping the bottom of the pan and bringing the outside edges to the middle. The scrambled eggs are cooked when they form soft creamy curds, but are barely set.

Remove from the heat, stir in the salmon, chives or dill and cream, if using, and pile the scrambled eggs on to the hot buttered toast on a warmed serving plate. Serve immediately.

Cook's Tips
Scrambled eggs should always be served immediately and should never have to wait for anyone.

Salmon slices, trimmings or off-cuts are excellent for this dish.

Preparation time
5 minutes

Cooking time
3–4 minutes

Serves 1

You will need
3 large eggs
1 tablespoon milk
15 g/½ oz butter
25–40 g/1–1½ oz smoked salmon, cut into narrow strips
1 teaspoon finely chopped chives or dill
1 tablespoon single cream (optional)
1–2 slices Irish Wheaten Bread (see page 115), toasted and buttered
salt and pepper

Wild Mushroom Omelette

Melt two-thirds of the butter in a small frying pan and cook the mushrooms until tender but holding their shape.

Put the eggs and the water into a small bowl, add the herbs and season with salt and pepper. Beat lightly with a fork to blend, then stir in the mushrooms.

Heat the remaining butter in a 20 cm/8 inch omelette or nonstick frying pan until it begins to foam. Pour in the egg mixture and quickly stir 3 or 4 times with a fork, then pull the egg from the edges of the pan into the centre, tilting the pan so that the liquid egg can flow towards the hot surface. The omelette is cooked when the egg looks set and is no longer liquid, but is still soft on top.

Using a spatula, fold the edge of the omelette closest to the frying pan handle towards the centre, then fold the opposite edge on top. Turn out on to a warmed plate, seam side down. Garnish with a sprig of parsley and serve immediately.

Cook's Tip
Use any mixture of edible wild mushrooms, such as chanterelles, horn of plenty, puff ball, parasols and field mushrooms. Do not wash the mushrooms as this will make them soggy, but use a pastry brush to clean them thoroughly, then slice or leave them whole, according to size.

Preparation time
10 minutes

Cooking time
5–8 minutes

Serves 1

You will need
25 g/1 oz butter
50 g/2 oz wild mushrooms, brushed, trimmed and sliced
3 eggs
1 teaspoon cold water
1 teaspoon finely chopped fresh herbs, e.g. parsley, chives and chervil
salt and pepper
sprig of flat leaf parsley, to garnish

Deep-Fried Wild Mushrooms in Batter with Garlic Mayonnaise

Mix the mayonnaise with the garlic and set aside.

Sift the flour and baking powder into a large mixing bowl, add the parsley, salt and pepper and make a well in the centre. Gradually add the water to make a smooth thick batter, beating well. Stir in the oil, mushrooms and onion.

Heat the oil for deep-frying to 180–190°C/350–375°F, or until a cube of bread browns in 30 seconds. Using a slotted spoon, lift the mushrooms from the batter and drop them into the hot oil, frying about 6 at a time. When the batter is just set underneath, carefully turn the mushrooms. Fry for 4–5 minutes, until crisp and golden. Drain on absorbent kitchen paper, pile on to 4 serving plates and serve immediately with the garlic mayonnaise.

Cook's Tip
This dish can also be made with cultivated mushrooms or a combination of cultivated and wild mushrooms.

Preparation time
10–15 minutes

Cooking time
4–5 minutes

Serves 4

You will need
150 ml/¼ pint mayonnaise
1–2 large garlic cloves, crushed
125 g/4 oz plain flour
½ teaspoon baking powder
1 tablespoon finely chopped parsley
150 ml/¼ pint water
1 teaspoon vegetable oil
375 g/12 oz mixed wild mushrooms, brushed and trimmed
½ small onion, very finely chopped
vegetable oil for deep-frying
salt and pepper

Grilled Mussels with Almonds and Herbs

Put the prepared mussels into a large saucepan, add 4 tablespoons water, bring to the boil, cover and cook over a high heat for 6–8 minutes, until the shells open. Remove the mussels from the pan and discard any unopened shells, along with the empty half-shells, leaving the mussels in the lower shell. Place the mussels in a shallow ovenproof dish.

Beat the butter and garlic together until soft, then stir in the almonds, breadcrumbs, parsley, lemon juice, and salt and pepper to taste. Divide this mixture between the mussels, covering the surface of each. Place under a preheated hot grill and cook until golden brown. Garnish with the lemon wedges and serve immediately, with Irish wheaten bread.

Cook's Tip
Clams can also be prepared and served in this way. Finely grated cheese, white wine or herbs of your choice, such as dill, chervil and chives, can be beaten into the butter for a slightly different flavour.

Preparation time
10–15 minutes

Cooking time
10–12 minutes

Serves 1–2

You will need
12 fresh, live, large mussels, washed, scraped, barnacles and beards removed (Cook's Tip, page 14)
50 g/2 oz butter
1 garlic clove, finely chopped
1 teaspoon finely chopped almonds
6 tablespoons fine white breadcrumbs
2 tablespoons finely chopped parsley
squeeze of lemon juice
salt and pepper
1–2 lemon wedges, to garnish
Irish Wheaten Bread (see page 115), to serve

Bookmaker's Sandwich

Slice the bread along one side and butter generously. Season the meat and cook quickly under a preheated hot grill or in a lightly oiled hot frying pan for 2–6 minutes, until cooked to your liking.

Place the steak inside the split and buttered bread, spread with mustard and serve immediately, with pickles if liked.

Cook's Tip
A soda farl (see page 120) makes an excellent alternative to the French bread. A soda farl also makes a suitable package for a fried egg, grilled sausage and rashers of bacon, when it is known as a soda sandwich – a most filling snack.

Preparation time
3 minutes

Cooking time
2–6 minutes

Serves 1

You will need
15–18 cm/6–7 inch length of French bread
25 g/1 oz butter
125–175 g/4–6 oz sirloin, fillet or rump steak, no more than 5 mm/¼ inch thick
1 tablespoon coarse grain mustard
salt and pepper

Oysters and Guinness

Open the oysters just before serving by holding each one firmly in a thick cloth, rounded side downwards. Insert a strong sharp knife, an old-fashioned pointed can opener, or a screwdriver into the hinge of the shell. Give a sharp twist upwards and prize off the shell. If you have difficulty opening the oysters from the hinge, try to prize the shells open by inserting the knife at the side of the shell. Take care not to lose the oyster juices.

Loosen the oyster, leaving it in the deep half of the shell with the juices. Arrange the oysters on a bed of crushed ice on a large serving plate. Serve with lemon wedges and a dusting of cayenne pepper if liked, bread and butter and a glass of creamy Guinness.

Cook's Tip
Oysters should be eaten like this only when bought fresh and alive from a good fishmonger. As long as the shells are tightly closed the oysters can be stored for several days if carefully packed in ice and well refrigerated.

Preparation time
5 minutes

Serves 1–2

You will need
6–12 fresh, tightly closed oysters, washed and scrubbed
crushed ice

To serve
1–2 thick lemon wedges
cayenne pepper (optional)
Irish Wheaten Bread (see page 115), buttered

Cockles and Mussels with Bacon

Put the prepared mussels in a large saucepan, add 300 ml/½ pint water, bring to the boil, cover and cook over a high heat for 5 minutes, shaking the pan occasionally during the cooking. Add the cockles and continue cooking for a further 3–5 minutes, until the shells open. Remove the cockles and mussels from the shells, discarding any unopened shells.

Cut the bacon rashers in half widthways. Roll each piece neatly and secure with a wooden cocktail stick. Place in a pan of boiling water for a few minutes to remove some of the salt and set the rolls. Drain, discard the cocktail sticks and pat the bacon rolls dry.

Melt the butter in a large frying pan and fry the bacon rolls until coloured; remove from the pan and keep warm. Fry the onion until soft, then add the mussels, cockles, herbs and seasoning. Toss in the butter to heat thoroughly. Divide between 4 warmed serving plates, scatter over the bacon rolls and garnish with a sprig of watercress. Serve immediately, with a glass of Guinness, if liked.

Cook's Tip
This can be made entirely with either mussels or cockles. To serve as a main course, double the quantities and serve with boiled potatoes.

Preparation time
30 minutes

Cooking time
8–10 minutes

Serves 4

You will need
about 2.5 kg/5 lb fresh, live mussels, washed, scrubbed, barnacles and beards removed (Cook's Tip, page 14)
about 375 g/12 oz cockles, washed and scrubbed
8 rashers of streaky bacon, rinded
50 g/2 oz butter
1 onion, finely chopped
2 tablespoons finely chopped parsley
1 teaspoon finely chopped chives
salt and pepper
4 sprigs of watercress, to garnish

Grilled Goats' Cheese on Soda Bread with Bacon and Tomatoes

Using a pastry cutter slightly larger than the diameter of the goats' cheese, cut a circle from each half of the soda farl. Toast the cut side until pale golden. Put a circle of cheese on top and place under a preheated hot grill for 3–4 minutes, until the cheese is beginning to melt and turning golden on top. Grill the tomato halves at the same time.

Meanwhile, heat the oil in a small frying pan and fry the bacon strips until crisp. Drain well on absorbent kitchen paper. Place the pieces of toasted bread and cheese in the centre of 2 serving plates. Arrange the tomatoes and bacon around the toasted cheese and sprinkle with the chives. Garnish with sprigs of chervil or dill.

Cook's Tips
Irish blue cheese such as Cashel Blue or Rathgore makes an excellent alternative to the goats' cheese. For a light lunch, serve 2 pieces of the grilled cheese per person, with a mixed leaf salad.

This is also excellent with cultivated or wild mushrooms cooked in a little butter and sprinkled among the bacon strips.

Preparation time
5 minutes

Cooking time
5–8 minutes

Serves 2

You will need
- 1 Soda Farl (see page 120), split in half horizontally
- 2 slices (1 cm/½ inch thick) cut from a cylindrical goats' cheese
- 4 rashers of back bacon, cut into 1 cm/½ inch strips
- 1 tablespoon oil
- 6 cherry tomatoes, halved
- 4–5 chives, cut into 2.5 cm/1 inch lengths
- 2 sprigs of chervil or dill, to garnish

The abundant variety of fish in Ireland's unpolluted waters around the coast and in the rivers and lakes, which attracted the first settlers, today draws fishermen and tourists from all over the world to sample the harvest. Throughout the country cooks prepare both modern and traditional dishes using the seasonal catch.

Fish and Seafood

Fried Herrings in Mustard and Oatmeal

Spread a little mustard inside each herring. Season the oatmeal with salt and pepper. Coat the fish in the beaten egg, then roll in the seasoned oatmeal, pressing it evenly over the fish.

Heat the fat or oil in a large frying pan and cook the herrings over a gentle heat for about 4 minutes on each side, until an even golden brown colour. Drain on absorbent kitchen paper, garnish with lemon wedges and watercress and serve with boiled new potatoes.

Cook's Tips
If the herrings are small allow 2 per person. If possible, ask the fishmonger to gut the herrings. To gut them yourself, first scrape off the scales, working from the tail to the head. Cut off the fins with a pair of kitchen scissors. Slit the belly from below the head to the vent and pull out the viscera. Run the point of a knife along the backbone to release any blood and wash under cold running water; dry well. It is traditional to serve herrings with the head on, although this can be removed before cooking. The backbone can also be removed and the herring flattened (see Cook's Tip, page 43) before being coated and fried, in which case fry the flesh side first.

Preparation time
15 minutes

Cooking time
8–10 minutes

Serves 4

You will need
1–2 tablespoons prepared English mustard
4 herrings, about 125 g/4 oz each, gutted, scaled, fins removed, washed and dried
75 g/3 oz oatmeal
1 egg, beaten
bacon fat or oil for frying
salt and pepper

To garnish
1 lemon, cut into 4 wedges
sprigs of watercress

Herb-Stuffed Herrings with Mustard Sauce

Use half the butter to grease a shallow ovenproof dish and a sheet of foil.

Melt the remaining butter in a saucepan and fry the onion until soft. Add the herbs, chopped eggs, lemon rind and breadcrumbs and season well with salt and pepper. Divide the stuffing between the 4 fish, re-shaping them carefully to make sure the stuffing does not fall out. Lay the herrings in the buttered dish, cover with the foil and place in a preheated oven at 160°C (325°F), Gas Mark 3 for 40–45 minutes.

While the fish is baking, prepare the sauce. Melt the butter in a saucepan, stir in the flour and gradually whisk in the milk to form a smooth paste. Simmer over a gentle heat for about 5 minutes, stirring all the time until the sauce is thick and the flour cooked. Stir in the lemon juice, mustard, parsley and salt and pepper to taste.

Serve the herrings hot with the mustard sauce and boiled new potatoes. Garnish with lemon wedges and flat leaf parsley.

Preparation time
15–20 minutes

Cooking time
40–45 minutes

Oven Temperature
160°C (325°F), Gas Mark 3

Serves 4–8

You will need
75 g/3 oz butter
1 small onion, finely chopped
2 tablespoons finely chopped parsley
1 teaspoon finely chopped dill
2 hard-boiled eggs, finely chopped
grated rind of ½ lemon
50 g/2 oz fresh breadcrumbs
4 herrings, about 125 g/4 oz each, prepared (Cook's Tip, page 40)
salt and pepper

Mustard sauce
25 g/1 oz butter
25 g/1 oz plain flour
300 ml/½ pint milk
1 tablespoon lemon juice
1 tablespoon prepared English mustard
1 tablespoon finely chopped parsley

To garnish
1 lemon, cut into 4 wedges
4 sprigs of flat leaf parsley

Potted Herrings

Lay the herrings flat, flesh side up and season well with salt and pepper. Roll up the fish from head to tail, flesh side inside. Secure with a wooden cocktail stick and pack tightly into a deep-sided, wide-bottomed pan.

Combine all the remaining ingredients in a saucepan and bring to the boil. Pour over the herrings and very gradually bring to simmering point. When the liquid is just moving, cover with a lid or foil, remove from the heat and leave overnight.

Serve cold, with salad, brown bread and butter and a glass of Guinness.

Cook's Tip
To bone and flatten a prepared herring, lay it flesh side down on a flat surface and press firmly along the backbone. Turn the fish over and ease the bones from the flesh by working your fingers along the backbone then lifting it towards the tail to release it.

Preparation time
15–20 minutes, plus standing overnight

Cooking time
1–2 minutes

Oven Temperature
160°C (325°F), Gas Mark 3

Serves 4–8

You will need
- 8 herrings, about 125 g/4 oz each, scaled, gutted, heads and tails removed, flattened and boned (Cook's Tip)
- 750 ml/1¼ pints vinegar
- 250 ml/8 fl oz water
- 8 whole cloves
- 175 g/6 oz onion, thinly sliced
- 3 large bay leaves
- 2 tablespoons pickling spice
- 4 blades of mace
- salt and pepper

Dublin Lawyer

Plunge the lobster, head first, into fast-boiling salted water for 2 minutes. Remove and hold under cold running water to stop the cooking. Place the lobster on a cutting board, shell down, and cut half lengthways. Remove and discard the grit bag near the head. Remove the meat from the shells and cut into chunks; reserve the shells. Remove and reserve the greenish liver (tomalley) and any coral (black when uncooked). Crack the claws and remove the meat.

Heat the butter in a large frying pan and fry the onion until soft. Add the lobster meat and fry until just cooked, then add the coral and liver. Warm the whiskey, pour over the lobster and flame. When the flames have died down, stir in the cream, mustard and lemon juice. Warm the reserved half-shells in boiling water, then pile in the lobster meat. Boil the cream mixture to reduce and thicken, season to taste with salt and pepper, pour over the lobster and serve immediately, garnished with lemon wedges and watercress.

Cook's Tip
Live lobster is required for this dish, since the final cooking takes place in the frying pan. There are several ways to kill a lobster, but if you can't face doing it yourself, ask your fishmonger, making sure that the lobster has no more than 2 minutes in boiling water.

Preparation time
20–30 minutes

Cooking time
20 minutes

Serves 2

You will need
1 live lobster, about 1 kg/2 lb
50 g/2 oz butter
1 small onion, finely chopped
4 tablespoons Irish whiskey
150 ml/¼ pint double cream
1 teaspoon prepared English mustard
1 teaspoon lemon juice
salt and pepper

To garnish
1 lemon, cut into 4 wedges
sprigs of watercress

Creamy Salmon Kedgeree

Use half the butter to grease an ovenproof dish and a sheet of foil.

Melt the remaining butter in a large frying pan and fry the onion until soft. Stir in the rice and season well. Add the salmon, eggs, parsley and cream, folding them carefully into the rice to prevent the fish and eggs from breaking up too much. Pile into the buttered dish, cover with the foil and place in a preheated oven at 180°C (350°F), Gas Mark 4 for 15 minutes. Serve hot, sprinkled with the chives.

Cook's Tips
Any white fish or smoked fish such as haddock or smoked salmon can be used to make the kedgeree. A combination of fresh and smoked salmon is particularly good.

The cream can be omitted but it helps to keep the dish moist.

Preparation time
15 minutes

Cooking time
15 minutes

Oven temperature
180°C (350°F), Gas Mark 4

Serves 4

You will need
50 g/2 oz butter
1 large onion, finely chopped
175 g/6 oz long-grain rice, boiled until just tender
500 g/1 lb cooked salmon, boned and broken into large flakes
3 hard-boiled eggs, roughly chopped
2 tablespoons finely chopped parsley
150 ml/¼ pint single cream
salt and pepper
1 teaspoon finely chopped chives, to garnish

Roast Fillet of Salmon with Saffron and Chive Cream Sauce

Heat a very little oil in a large frying pan. Season the salmon with salt and pepper and place flesh side down in the hot oil. Cook over a high heat for about 2 minutes to brown. Transfer to a lightly oiled baking sheet, skin side down, season and finish cooking in a preheated oven at 240°C (475°F), Gas Mark 9 for about 7–9 minutes, depending on the thickness of the fillet. The flesh should turn opaque when cooked.

While the fish is roasting, make the sauce. Combine the stock, wine and saffron in a saucepan and reduce by half. Add the cream, bring to the boil and boil until the sauce thickens and coats the back of a spoon.

Place the fish in the centre of 4 large warmed serving plates, pour the sauce around and sprinkle with chives. Serve with steamed seasonal vegetables and boiled new potatoes.

Cook's Tip
Fish stock: for 1.2 litres/2 pints stock, sweat 250 g/8 oz chopped onions or shallots in butter until soft, add 500 g/1 lb washed white fish bones and trimmings. Pour on 150 ml/¼ pint dry white wine, 1 litre/1¾ pints water and the juice of 1 lemon. Simmer for 20 minutes. Strain before use.

Preparation time
2–5 minutes

Cooking time
9–11 minutes

Oven temperature
240°C (475°F), Gas Mark 9

Serves 4

You will need
a little vegetable oil
4 pieces salmon fillet, about 150–175 g/5–6 oz each
salt and pepper
1–2 tablespoons snipped chives

Sauce
150 ml/¼ pint fish stock (Cook's Tip)
150 ml/¼ pint dry white wine
4 saffron threads
150 ml/¼ pint single cream

Smoked Fish Pie

Put the haddock in a shallow saucepan, pour on the milk, bring slowly to simmering point and simmer for 5–10 minutes.

Meanwhile, melt the butter in a saucepan and fry the onion until soft but not coloured. Add the mushrooms and continue to fry until lightly browned. Stir in the flour and cook gently for about 1 minute, then remove from the heat.

When the fish is cooked, strain the milk into a jug and gradually add to the onion and mushroom mixture, stirring well. Bring to the boil and simmer for 10 minutes until thick, stirring continually. Add the mustard, parsley, lemon juice, eggs and seasoning. Flake the fish, discarding the bones, and add to the sauce. Pile into a deep ovenproof pie dish.

Mash the potatoes with the melted butter and milk, season well and pile on top of the fish mixture, covering it evenly. Scatter over the cheese and place in a preheated oven at 190°C (375°F), Gas Mark 5, until piping hot and crisp.

Cook's Tips
When using smoked fish, always buy undyed fish.

For extra flavour, add 6 peppercorns, 1 blade of mace, 1 bay leaf, a slice of onion and 2 cloves to the milk while cooking the fish.

Preparation time
20–30 minutes

Cooking time
35–40 minutes

Oven temperature
190°C (375°F), Gas Mark 5

Serves 4–6

You will need
500 g/1 lb smoked haddock
450 ml/¾ pint milk
50 g/2 oz butter
1 onion, finely chopped
175 g/6 oz mushrooms, sliced
25 g/1 oz plain flour
1 teaspoon prepared English mustard
2 tablespoons finely chopped parsley
1 tablespoon lemon juice
2–3 hard-boiled eggs, roughly chopped
salt and pepper

Potato topping
875 g/1¾ lb potatoes, freshly boiled
25 g/1 oz butter, melted
3–4 tablespoons milk
50 g/2 oz Cheddar cheese, grated

Poached Salmon Steaks with Dill Butter

Put the water, wine, vinegar, onion, carrot, bouquet garni and peppercorns into a saucepan. Bring to the boil, then reduce the heat, cover and simmer for 30 minutes. Cool slightly.

Place the salmon steaks in a large, shallow frying pan or fireproof dish. Strain enough of the flavoured liquid over the salmon to barely cover. Bring to simmering point, cover and simmer gently for 5–8 minutes, until the flesh is opaque.

Lift the salmon steaks carefully from the cooking liquid and drain on absorbent kitchen paper. Melt the butter and stir in the dill. Serve the salmon on warmed plates with a little dill butter poured over. Garnish with lemon wedges and watercress and serve with boiled new potatoes and steamed seasonal vegetables.

Cook's Tip
The salmon steaks can be poached in water with white wine, lemon juice and herbs, without the liquid being simmered for 30 minutes; however, the flavour of the finished dish will not be as good.

Hollandaise sauce (see page 25), either plain or with finely chopped herbs, is an excellent alternative to dill butter and is the traditional accompaniment to Irish poached salmon.

Preparation time
30 minutes

Cooking time
5–10 minutes

Serves 4

You will need
1.2 litres/2 pints water
300 ml/½ pint dry white wine
50 ml/2 fl oz tarragon vinegar
1 small onion, sliced
1 small carrot, sliced
bouquet garni (Cook's Tip, page 10)
12 peppercorns
4 salmon steaks, about
175–250 g/6–8 oz each
(2–2.5 cm/¾–1 inch thick)
125 g/4 oz butter
2 tablespoons finely chopped dill

To garnish
1 lemon, cut into 4 wedges
sprigs of watercress

Cold Boiled Lobster with Herb Mayonnaise

Remove the claws from the lobster, crack and reserve. Place the lobster on a cutting board, shell side down, extend the tail and cut the lobster in half lengthways. Discard the grit bag near the head, the feathery gills and the dark intestinal vein running down the centre of the tail. Rub the greyish-green liver and the pink roe (coral) through a sieve into a mixing bowl. Add the egg, herbs, capers, mayonnaise and lemon juice to taste, stirring to combine.

Remove the flesh from the tail shells and cut into slanting slices. Put into a bowl and add enough of the mayonnaise mixture to moisten. Return to the shell halves and add a little extra mayonnaise to garnish.

Arrange half a lobster on each plate, garnish with a cracked claw, a lemon wedge and watercress. Serve with a mixed leaf salad, the remaining herb mayonnaise and buttered bread.

Cook's Tip
When buying any shellfish it is important that they are very fresh. If possible, buy them live and cook them yourself. To cook a lobster, plunge it head first into fast-boiling, well-salted water, hold down with tongs and boil for 1½ minutes, then simmer for 8–10 minutes per 500 g/1 lb to cook the flesh.

Preparation time
15–20 minutes

Serves 2

You will need
1 cooked lobster, about 1 kg/2¼ lb
1 hard-boiled egg, sieved
2 tablespoons finely chopped parsley
2 tablespoons finely chopped chervil
1 teaspoon finely chopped chives
1 tablespoon finely chopped capers
150 ml/¼ pint thick mayonnaise
lemon juice

To garnish
lemon wedges
sprigs of watercress

Dressed Crab

Preparation time
30 minutes

Cooking time
25 minutes

Serves 1

You will need
1 live crab, about 875 g/1¾ lb
2–3 tablespoons fine fresh white breadcrumbs
¼–½ teaspoon English mustard
squeeze of lemon juice
1 hard-boiled egg, white chopped, yolk sieved
1–2 tablespoons finely chopped parsley
salt and pepper

To garnish
lemon wedges
sprigs of watercress

Plunge the live crab into a large pan of boiling salted water, cover and simmer for 25 minutes. Remove from the water and leave until cold.

Lay the crab on its back, twist off the legs and claws. Remove and discard the bony tail flap. Lever off the central body, pulling it away from the shell. The body consists of bone with some white crab meat and the 'dead men's fingers'. Discard the 'fingers', the stomach sac from behind the mouth and the mouth itself. Cut the body in half and use a skewer to pick out the white meat from the crevices. Put the meat into a bowl.

Crack the claws and legs, extract the meat and combine with the reserved white meat.

Scoop out the soft yellowish-brown meat from inside the shell and put in a second bowl. Wash and dry the shell. Cream the brown meat, adding the breadcrumbs, mustard and salt and pepper to taste, then arrange down the centre of the shell. Season the white meat with salt, pepper and lemon juice and pile into the shell on either side of the brown meat.

Decorate with the egg and parsley, garnish with lemon and watercress and serve with mayonnaise, salad and brown bread and butter.

Cook's Tip
It is best to cook your own crab; it will have a better flavour and you will know it is fresh. Buy cooked crabs only from a good fishmonger with a high turnover. Small heavy crabs will have plenty of meat.

To use the shell as a container, enlarge the opening by breaking away the shell along the line of weakness that runs around the rim.

Cod and Prawn Bake in Cheese Sauce

Put the milk into a saucepan with the onion, peppercorns, mace, bay leaf and parsley stalks. Bring to the boil, then remove from the heat and leave to infuse.

Melt the butter in another saucepan and use a little to brush the inside of an ovenproof pie dish. Cut the cod into finger-sized strips, place in the pie dish and scatter the mushrooms and prawns on top.

Add the flour to the butter in the saucepan, stirring to blend. Strain the flavoured milk and gradually stir into the flour mixture to make a smooth sauce. Bring to the boil, stirring continually, until the sauce thickens. Season with salt, pepper and lemon juice and add two-thirds of the cheese. Stir until the cheese melts, then pour over the fish, sprinkle with the remaining cheese and place in a preheated oven at 180°C (350°F), Gas Mark 4 for 20–25 minutes, until golden brown. Serve with Irish Wheaten Bread (see page 115) and salad.

Cook's Tip

Any firm-fleshed fish or shellfish can be used for this dish, and either wild or cultivated mushrooms. The bake can also be made in 4 individual (300 ml/½ pint) pie dishes, or in 8 scallop shells, as a first course.

Preparation time
15 minutes

Cooking time
20–25 minutes

Oven temperature
180°C (350°F), Gas Mark 4

Serves 4

You will need

450 ml/¾ pint milk
slice of onion
6 peppercorns
1 blade of mace
1 bay leaf
4–6 parsley stalks
50 g/2 oz butter
450 g/1 lb cod, skinned and filleted
50 g/2 oz button mushrooms, sliced
125 g/4 oz cooked peeled prawns
40 g/1½ oz plain flour
1 tablespoon lemon juice
125 g/4 oz Cheddar cheese, grated
salt and pepper

Grilled Mackerel with Gooseberry and Fennel Sauce

Season the mackerel inside and out and stuff with the fennel sprigs and stalks if using. Cut 2–3 diagonal slits on each side of the fish so that the heat can penetrate more quickly. Brush the fish lightly with oil and place on a lightly oiled baking sheet.

To make the sauce, put the gooseberries and the water in a large saucepan. Bring to the boil, then add the sugar, butter and fennel. Cook gently for 6–7 minutes, until the berries burst, without letting them cook to a pulp.

While the sauce is cooking, place the mackerel under a hot grill and cook for 4–7 minutes on each side, depending on the size, turning very carefully. Remove the fennel from inside the fish and serve immediately, garnished with lemon wedges and sprigs of fresh fennel. Serve with the hot gooseberry sauce and boiled new potatoes.

Cook's Tip
Mackerel is a very oily fish and needs a sharp sauce to offset the richness of the flesh. Gooseberry or another tart fruit such as rhubarb is traditional; sorrel also makes a good sauce, or try a Mustard Sauce (see page 41). Herrings may also be cooked in this way.

Preparation time
5–10 minutes

Cooking time
8–15 minutes

Serves 4

You will need
4 small mackerel, about 275 g/9 oz each, gutted, washed and dried
sprigs of fresh fennel (optional)
oil for brushing
salt and pepper

Gooseberry sauce
375 g/12 oz gooseberries, topped and tailed
125 ml/4 fl oz water
2 tablespoons granulated sugar
25 g/1 oz butter
1 tablespoon finely chopped fennel

To garnish
1 lemon, cut into 4 wedges
4 sprigs of fennel

Cockle and Mussel Pie

Fry the vegetables in the butter until soft. Add the mussels, wine and stock or water. Bring to the boil, cover the pan and cook for 3 minutes, add the cockles and cook for a further 3–5 minutes, until all the shells have opened. Remove the shells from the pan, discarding any that remain closed. Reserve the cooking liquid and remove the fish from the shells.

Mix the butter and flour together to form a paste and gradually whisk into the hot cooking liquid until it thickens. Add the parsley and season with salt and pepper. Stir in the mussels and cockles and divide between 4 ovenproof cups, soup bowls or individual pie dishes (about 175–200 ml/6–7 fl oz each).

Roll out the pastry on a lightly floured surface and cut out 4 lids for the pies. Cut leaf shapes from the trimmings. Brush the rims of the cups or bowls with beaten egg and top with the pastry lids. Brush lightly with egg, decorate with the pastry leaves and glaze the leaves with a little more egg. Place in a preheated oven at 200°C (400°C) Gas Mark 6 for 12–15 minutes, until golden brown. Serve immediately.

Cook's Tip
Canned smoked mussels, oysters and cockles can be used instead of the fresh fish; reduce the liquid by 150 ml/¼ pint and add the fish to the sauce just before baking.

Preparation time
30 minutes

Cooking time
12–15 minutes

Oven temperature
200°C (400°F), Gas Mark 6

Serves 4

You will need
1 garlic clove, finely chopped
1 onion, finely chopped
2 small leeks, finely diced
1 carrot, finely diced
2 celery sticks, finely diced
175 g/6 oz mushrooms, sliced
50 g/2 oz butter
24 fresh, live mussels, prepared (Cook's Tip, page 14)
300 ml/½ pint dry white wine
150 ml/¼ pint fish stock (Cook's Tip, page 45) or water
48 cockles, scrubbed
15 g/½ oz butter
15 g/½ oz plain flour
2 tablespoons finely chopped parsley
300 g/10 oz puff pastry, thawed if frozen
beaten egg, to glaze
salt and pepper

Baked Trout with Herb Stuffing and Cream Sauce

Melt 50 g/2 oz of the butter in a large frying pan and fry the onion until soft but not coloured. Remove from the heat. Mix the herbs together and add half to the pan, along with the breadcrumbs, lemon rind and juice, nutmeg and salt and pepper. Mix well and moisten with 1–2 tablespoons of the cream. Divide the mixture into 4 and use it to stuff the fish.

Butter a large ovenproof baking dish with half the remaining butter. Lay the stuffed trout head to tail in the dish, dot with the last of the butter and pour over the wine. Place in a preheated oven at 240°C (475°F), Gas Mark 9 for 20 minutes, until slightly firm to the touch.

Strain the cooking liquid into a saucepan and boil rapidly to reduce by half. Add the remaining cream and herbs and return to the boil. Taste and adjust the seasoning if necessary.

Arrange the fish on 4 warmed serving plates, pour a little sauce around each fish and serve with boiled new potatoes and crisp green vegetables or salad.

Cook's Tip
Brown trout are freshwater fish, native to Ireland's rivers, lakes and streams. They are fine and delicate, with a slightly nutty flavour.

Preparation time
20 minutes

Cooking time
20 minutes

Oven temperature
240°C (475°F), Gas Mark 9

Serves 4

You will need
75 g/3 oz butter
1 small onion, finely chopped
2 tablespoons finely chopped parsley
1 tablespoon finely chopped chives
3 teaspoons finely chopped dill
50 g/2 oz fresh white breadcrumbs
finely grated rind of ½ lemon
2 teaspoons lemon juice
pinch of ground nutmeg
250 ml/8 fl oz single cream
4 rainbow or brown trout, about 300–325 g/10–11 oz each, gutted, washed and dried, heads and tails left on
150 ml/¼ pint dry white wine
salt and pepper

Fried Trout with Toasted Hazelnuts and Herbs

Season the fish inside and out and toss in the flour, shaking off any excess. Fry in half the butter until golden brown, about 5 minutes on each side. Turn carefully, once only, to prevent the skin from breaking.

While the trout are cooking, toast the hazelnuts lightly under a medium-hot grill, turning frequently. Rub off the skins, then roughly chop the nuts. Transfer the cooked trout to 4 warmed serving plates. Scatter the nuts over the fish and keep warm.

Melt the remaining butter in a small saucepan, allow it to foam and turn golden brown, then add the lemon juice. Pour the browned butter over the trout, scatter over the herbs and garnish with lemon wedges and watercress. Serve with boiled new potatoes and green vegetables or salad.

Cook's Tip
To clarify butter, put it in a small saucepan, bring to the boil and allow to bubble for about 10 seconds, without browning. Remove from the heat, leave to settle, then carefully pour through a sieve lined with damp muslin, leaving the milky residue in the pan. This will remove all the salty sediment which causes butter to burn.

Preparation time
10–15 minutes

Cooking time
6–8 minutes

Serves 4

You will need
4 trout, about 300–325 g/10–11oz each, gutted, washed and dried, heads and tails left on
125 g/4 oz plain flour
250 g/8 oz butter, clarified (Cook's Tip)
125 g/4 oz hazelnuts, shelled
2 tablespoons lemon juice
2 tablespoons finely chopped parsley
1 tablespoon finely chopped chives
salt and pepper

To garnish
1 lemon, cut into 4 wedges
sprigs of watercress

The lush green pastures of Ireland have always been noted for the production of the finest beef and lamb. Pigs are easier to keep and their meat – either as fresh pork or cured as bacon or ham – has been more widely available over the centuries. A meal today is generally considered incomplete if there is no meat on the plate.

Meat

Fillet Steak with Cashel Blue Cheese and Croûtons

Trim the cheese and cut to cover the top of the fillet steak. Heat the butter in a small frying pan, season the steak with salt and pepper and seal on both sides in the butter.

Transfer the steak to a buttered baking sheet and put the cheese on top. Place in a preheated oven at 220°C (425°F), Gas Mark 7 for 5 minutes for rare steak, 8 minutes for medium rare and 15 minutes for well done, allowing the cheese to melt and lightly colour.

Transfer the steak to a warmed serving plate, scatter round the croûtons and sprigs of thyme, pour around the cooking juices and garnish with the watercress. Serve immediately.

Preparation time
5 minutes

Cooking time
5–15 minutes

Oven temperature
220°C (425°F), Gas Mark 7

Serves 1

You will need

50 g/2 oz Cashel Blue cheese, rind removed
1 fillet steak, about 200–250 g/7–8 oz, cut 4 cm/1½ inches thick
25 g/1 oz butter
5 g/¼ oz croûtons (Cook's Tip, page 10)
few sprigs of thyme
salt and pepper
watercress, to garnish

Steak and Kidney Pie

Trim the beef and cut into 2.5 cm/1 inch cubes. Skin, core and cube the kidney. Toss all the meat in the seasoned flour and fry in a little hot oil until browned. Transfer to a saucepan. Fry the onion in the oil until soft, add the mushrooms and continue to fry until lightly browned. Add to the meat, with the stock, stout, bay leaf and parsley. Bring to the boil, then simmer for 1½–2 hours, until the meat is almost tender. Taste and adjust the seasoning and leave until cold.

Put a pie funnel in the centre of a 900 ml/1½ pint rimmed pie dish. Turn the cold stew into the dish. Roll out the pastry thinly and cut out a lid for the pie dish and a 1 cm/½ inch strip to go around the rim. Brush the rim of the dish with beaten egg, lay the pastry strip around the rim and brush again with egg. Cover with the pastry lid, pressing to seal the edges well. Decorate with pastry trimmings. Brush with beaten egg and place in a preheated oven at 220°C (425°F), Gas Mark 7 for 25–35 minutes, until the pastry is risen and golden in colour. Serve immediately.

Cook's Tip
Any good cut of stewing beef can be used, such as chuck steak and thick plate.

Red wine can be used instead of the stout.

Preparation time
30 minutes

Cooking time
2–2½ hours

Oven temperature
220°C (425°F), Gas Mark 7

Serves 4–6

You will need

750 g/1½ lb topside of beef
125 g/4 oz ox or lamb's kidney
50 g/2 oz plain flour, seasoned
vegetable oil for frying
1 large onion, finely chopped
125 g/4 oz mushrooms, sliced
150 ml/¼ pint beef stock
150 ml/¼ pint Irish dry stout
1 bay leaf
1–2 tablespoons chopped parsley
300 g/10 oz puff or flaky pastry, thawed if frozen
salt and pepper
beaten egg, to glaze

Boiled Silverside with Dumplings

Heat a little oil in a large saucepan and brown the meat on all sides. Add the cloved onion, herbs, water and stout. Bring to the boil, then simmer for 1½ hours.

Meanwhile, make the dumplings. Sift the flour into a bowl, stir in the suet, herbs and seasoning, then mix to a sticky dough with the egg and water.

Remove the cloved onion and herbs from the simmering liquid, add the pickling onions and carrots, and drop in spoonfuls of the dumpling dough. Simmer for a further 30 minutes, until the meat is tender.

Serve the meat on a hot dish, surrounded by the vegetables and dumplings. Accompany by boiled potatoes and some of the cooking liquid in a sauceboat.

Cook's Tip
Topside of beef can replace the silverside, with the same cooking time. Boned and rolled brisket, sometimes called top breast, can also be used, but it takes 4–5 hours to cook.

Preparation time
20–30 minutes

Cooking time
2 hours

Serves 6

You will need
vegetable oil for frying
1½–2 kg/3½–4 lb silverside of beef, tied neatly
1 onion, stuck with 6 cloves
4–5 parsley stalks, 1 bay leaf, 5 cm/2 inch piece of celery stick, tied together
600 ml/1 pint water
300 ml/½ pint Irish dry stout
12–16 small pickling onions, peeled
500 g/1 lb small carrots, peeled

Dumplings
125 g/4 oz self-raising flour
50 g/2 oz shredded suet
2 tablespoons finely chopped parsley
1 egg (size 2), beaten with 4 tablespoons cold water

Ulster Steak

Toss the meat in the seasoned flour and brown well on all sides in the hot oil in a large frying pan. Transfer to a flame-proof casserole. Fry the mushrooms in the oil for a few minutes to colour slightly, then add to the meat with the onion, mushroom ketchup, brown sauce, the remaining flour and the water or stock. Bring to the boil, cover and simmer for 1½–2 hours, until the meat is tender. Add a little extra water if the liquid reduces too much.

Serve hot, with mashed potatoes, Champ (see page 92) or fresh Soda Bread (see pages 14–115) to mop up the sauce.

Cook's Tip
Sliced carrots can be added together with the onion and stout can be used instead of water or stock.

Preparation time
15–20 minutes

Cooking time
1½–2 hours

Serves 4–5

You will need
750 g–1 kg/1½–2 lb topside of beef, cut into individual portions, 1.5 cm/¾ inch thick
50 g/2 oz plain flour, seasoned
vegetable oil for frying
175 g/6 oz button mushrooms
1 large onion, sliced
2 teaspoons mushroom ketchup
1 tablespoon brown sauce
900 ml/1½ pint water or beef stock
salt and pepper

Roast Fillet of Lamb with Cabbage and Wild Mushrooms

Cut the meat into 4 pieces, season well with salt and pepper. Heat the oil in a small roasting dish and fry the lamb until sealed on all sides. Put the lamb in a preheated oven at 220°C (425°F), Gas Mark 7 and roast for 10–12 minutes for medium rare lamb, 15 minutes for medium and 20 minutes for well done. Remove from the oven and keep warm.

While the lamb is cooking, boil the cabbage until tender, drain, toss in half the butter, season well and keep warm. Fry the diced bacon in the remaining butter until lightly browned, add the mushrooms and fry until cooked. Keep warm.

Discard the fat from the roasting dish and pour in the wine and port. Bring to the boil, stirring continually. Pour over the mushrooms and bacon, taste and season with salt and pepper if necessary.

Divide the cabbage between 4 warmed serving plates, piling it in the centre of each plate. Cut each piece of lamb in half and arrange on top of the cabbage. Scatter the mushrooms, bacon and a little of the wine sauce around the edge. Garnish with chervil and serve immediately.

Preparation time
30 minutes

Cooking time
10–20 minutes

Cooking temperature
220°C (425°F), Gas Mark 7

Serves 4

You will need

1 lamb fillet, about 500 g/1 lb, trimmed to leave only a thin layer of fat along one side
vegetable oil for frying
1 small green cabbage, finely shredded
125 g/4 oz butter
125 g/4 oz unsmoked back bacon, diced
175 g/6 oz mixed wild mushrooms, cleaned and sliced if large
50 ml/2 fl oz red wine
2 tablespoons port
salt and pepper
sprigs of chervil, to garnish

Individual Beef Wellington

Trim the fillet steaks, tie neatly and fry in the butter until sealed on both sides and browned. Remove from the pan and leave until completely cold before removing the string.

Roll out the pastry to a rectangle 40 x 33 cm/16 x 13 inches. Cut a strip for decoration 2.5cm/1 inch from the narrow side and divide the remaining pastry into 4. Roll out each piece to about 3mm/⅛ inch thick.

Spread the pâté evenly over the 4 steaks. Place a steak on one side of each piece of pastry, brush the edges with the beaten egg and fold over the remaining pastry to form a neat parcel, cutting away excess pastry where necessary and sealing the edges together. Place on a damp baking sheet, decorate with shapes cut from the pastry strip, brush with beaten egg and bake in a preheated oven at 220°C (425°F), Gas Mark 7, until the pastry is risen and golden and the meat cooked to your liking: 20 minutes for medium-rare, 25 minutes for well done. Serve immediately, garnished with watercress.

Cook's Tip
To avoid soggy pastry, make sure that the meat has been well sealed and is quite cold before wrapping in the pastry. For well-cooked meat, the steaks can be almost completely cooked in the frying pan before wrapping in the pastry.

Preparation time
30 minutes

Cooking time
25–30 minutes

Oven temperature
220°C (425°F), Gas Mark 7

Serves 4

You will need
4 fillet steaks, about 175–250 g/6–8 oz each, cut about 2.5cm/1 inch thick
25 g/1 oz butter
500 g/1 lb puff pastry, thawed if frozen
175 g/6 oz Chicken Liver Pâté (see page 24)
1 egg, beaten
watercress, to garnish

Beef and Guinness Stew

Toss the meat in the seasoned flour and fry in hot oil in a large saucepan or flameproof casserole until brown. Add the onion and cook for a few minutes, then stir in any remaining flour. Add the carrot, Guinness and water, stirring well to combine. Bring to the boil, add the bay leaf, cover and simmer gently for 1–1½ hours, until the meat is tender. Alternatively cook in a preheated oven at 150–160°C (300–325°F) Gas Mark 2–3.

Add the prunes and cook for a further 30 minutes. Remove the bay leaf, taste and adjust the seasoning, sprinkle with the parsley and serve hot, with potatoes boiled in their skins.

Cook's Tip
Chuck steak or shin of beef can also be used for this stew.

Preparation time
20–30 minutes

Cooking time
1½–2 hours

Oven temperature
150–160°C (300–325°F), Gas Mark 2–3

Serves 4

You will need
1 kg/2 lb topside of beef, cut into 2.5cm/1 inch cubes
50 g/2 oz plain flour, seasoned
vegetable oil for frying
1 large onion, sliced
1 large carrot,thickly sliced
300 ml/½ pint Guinness
750 ml/1¼ pints water
1 bay leaf
125 g/4 oz prunes, soaked in water
2 tablespoons finely chopped parsley
salt and pepper

Oxtail Stew

Fry the oxtail in the hot oil until well browned on all sides, then transfer to a flameproof casserole. Fry the onion in the oil until brown, and add to the oxtail with the flour and tomato purée. Pour on the liquid and stir to blend. Add the carrots, thyme, bay leaf, mace, salt and pepper and bring to the boil. Cover, reduce the heat and simmer very gently for 3–3½ hours, until the meat is tender and falling off the bones. Alternatively the stew can be cooked in a preheated oven at 150–160°C (300–325°F) Gas Mark 2–3.

Skim off the excess fat, taste and adjust the seasoning and serve with mashed potatoes, Champ (see page 92) or potatoes boiled in their skins. Steamed celery and broccoli are excellent accompaniments.

Cook's Tip
Oxtail stew can be quite fatty. For the best results it should be made the day before, left to cool and refrigerated overnight. The fat will solidify on top of the stew and can be lifted off before the stew is reheated.

Preparation time
20–30 minutes

Cooking time
3–3½ hours

Oven temperature
150–160°C (300–325°F), Gas Mark 2–3

Serves 4–6

You will need
- 1 large oxtail, about 1.5 kg/3 lb, cut into 5 cm/2 inch lengths
- vegetable oil for frying
- 1 large onion, sliced
- 50 g/2 oz plain flour
- 2 tablespoons tomato purée
- 1.5 litres/2½ pints beef stock water, Guinness or red wine
- 2 large carrots, sliced
- sprig of thyme
- 1 bay leaf
- pinch of ground mace
- salt and pepper

Minced Beef Stew

Fry the onion in the hot oil until soft but not coloured. Add the beef and continue to fry over a high heat until browned. Stir in the tomato purée, brown sauce, carrot and stock or water. Bring to the boil, cover, then simmer for about 30 minutes, until the meat is cooked and the carrot is tender.

Blend the arrowroot with a little of the cooking liquid and stir into the stew to thicken. Add the parsley and season to taste with salt and pepper. Serve hot, with boiled, baked or mashed potatoes and fresh garden peas.

Cook's Tip
Instead of, or as well as, the carrot, you could use parsnips, turnips, celery or leek.

This mince stew is often used as the basis for a pie, either with a potato topping or with a pastry crust, in which case it should be left until cold before filling the pastry.

Preparation time
15 minutes

Cooking time
30 minutes

Serves 4

You will need
- 1 large onion, finely chopped
- vegetable oil for frying
- 500 g/1 lb minced beef
- 2 tablespoons tomato purée
- 2 tablespoons brown sauce
- 1 large carrot, diced
- 350 ml/12 fl oz beef stock or water
- 1 teaspoon arrowroot
- 1 tablespoon finely chopped parsley
- salt and pepper

Stuffed Pocket of Steak

Fry the onion in half the butter until soft but not coloured, add the mushrooms and continue to fry until both are cooked and beginning to colour. Stir in the ham, breadcrumbs, parsley and salt and pepper to taste. Leave until cold.

Fill the pocket in the steak with the cold stuffing and stitch the open edges together with fine string.

Heat the grill and grill rack to very hot. Brush the rack lightly with oil, place the steak on top, dot with half the remaining butter, season with freshly ground black pepper and cook for approximately 5–10 minutes each side for medium rare and 10–20 minutes each side for well done, adding the remaining butter and more seasoning on turning. Remove the string and cut into 1 cm/½ inch slices. Serve with the cooking juices or herb butter, with grilled tomatoes and jacket potatoes.

Cook's Tips

The steak can be stuffed in advance and stored in the refrigerator until ready to grill.

After the steak has been browned and sealed under the grill it can be finished in a preheated oven at 220°C (425°F), Gas Mark 7.

Preparation time
15–20 minutes

Cooking time
15–30 minutes

Serves 4

You will need

3 tablespoons finely chopped onion
50 g/2 oz butter
175 g/ 6 oz mushrooms, finely chopped
50 g/2 oz cooked ham, finely chopped
25 g/1 oz fine fresh white breadcrumbs
2 tablespoons finely chopped parsley
about 1 kg/2 lb middle cut rump steak in one piece, about 4 cm/1½ inches thick, with a pocket cut along its length
salt and pepper

An Ulster Fry

Fry the sausages in a little oil until almost cooked then add the bacon rashers and black or white pudding and fry until cooked. Remove from the pan, drain on absorbent kitchen paper and keep warm. Fry all the breads until lightly toasted, drain and keep warm.

Add a little extra oil to the pan, and fry the eggs, spooning the hot fat over the yolk and white until cooked to your liking. Arrange all the fried ingredients on a warmed serving plate, garnish with the watercress and serve immediately.

Cook's Tip
An Ulster Fry differs from an Irish Fry and a British Fry mainly in that it includes a selection of fried traditional breads. It is served at any time of the day – for breakfast, lunch, high tea or supper, or as a snack. Mushrooms, tomatoes, onions, liver, chops and potatoes can be added for a more substantial meal!

Preparation time
5 minutes

Cooking time
15 minutes

Serves 1

You will need
1–2 sausages
vegetable oil for frying
2 rashers of bacon, back and streaky, rinded
2 slices of black or white pudding
½ Soda Farl (see page 120)
1 Potato Cake, halved (see page 28)
1 Pancake, halved (see page 115)
1–2 eggs
watercress, to garnish

Irish Meat Loaf

Grease a 19 x 9 cm/7½ x 3½ inch loaf tin with half the butter and dust with the breadcrumbs.

Fry the onion in the remaining butter until soft, add the minced beef and cook until browned. Stir in all the remaining ingredients and pack tightly into the prepared tin. Cover with foil and bake in a preheated oven at 190°C (375°F), Gas Mark 5 for 1–1½ hours, until firm to the touch.

Leave in the tin for 10–15 minutes before turning out. Serve hot or cold, cut in slices. A rich tomato sauce (Cook's Tip) is a tasty accompaniment.

Cook's Tips
To make dried breadcrumbs, toast fresh white breadcrumbs in the oven until dry and golden brown.

This same mixture can be used to make meatballs. Cook them in this spicy tomato sauce: fry 1 chopped onion and 1 chopped garlic clove until soft, then add 425 g/14 oz canned plum tomatoes, 65 ml/2½ fl oz stock and a pinch of sugar, basil, ground cinnamon and seasoning; simmer for 20 minutes.

Preparation time
15–20 minutes

Cooking time
1–1¼ hours

Oven temperature
190°C (375°F), Gas Mark 5

Serves 4

You will need
50 g/2 oz butter
25 g/1 oz dried breadcrumbs (Cook's Tip)
1 small onion, finely chopped
500 g/1 lb minced beef
125 g/4 oz white breadcrumbs
1 tablespoon tomato ketchup
1 teaspoon Worcestershire sauce
1 teaspoon crushed juniper berries
1 tablespoon finely chopped chives
1 tablespoon finely chopped parsley
1 teaspoon finely chopped oregano
1 egg, beaten
salt and pepper

Pressed Ox Tongue

Put the tongue into a large saucepan, cover with fresh cold water and bring to the boil. Discard this first water, then rinse the tongue, wash out the pan and begin again with fresh water, this time adding the onion stuck with the cloves, the peppercorns, carrot, celery and herbs. Bring to the boil and simmer for 4 hours, until cooked and very tender.

Leave the tongue to cool slightly in the liquid, then remove and plunge into a bowl of cold water, reserving the cooking liquid. Peel off the skin and remove the root and small bones. Curl the tongue round to fit very tightly into a tongue press, a deep round cake tin or deep,straight-sided dish.

Put the gelatine in a cup, moisten with a little cold water, then set in a saucepan of hot water and stir until clear. Mix with 275 ml/9 fl oz of the strained cooking liquid, pour over the tongue, cover and press down with weights. Leave in the refrigerator overnight to set. Turn out and serve, thinly sliced.

Cook's Tip
To test whether the tongue is cooked, try to pull out the small bone at the base of the tongue; if it comes away easily the tongue is cooked. For a further test, pierce the thickest part of the tongue, just above the root, with a skewer; if it slips in easily the tongue is ready.

Preparation time
10–15 minutes, plus overnight pressing

Cooking time
4–5 hours

Serves 6

You will need
1 salted ox tongue, 1.5–3 kg/3–6 lb, soaked overnight in cold water
1 large onion, stuck with 5 cloves
6–8 peppercorns
1 large carrot, halved
2 celery sticks, halved
2 bay leaves
a few parsley stalks
a sprig of thyme
2 teaspoons gelatine powder

Irish Stew

Layer the meat and vegetables in a deep saucepan or flameproof casserole, sprinkling half the parsley between the layers and seasoning each layer with salt and pepper; finish with a layer of potatoes. Pour in the stock or water and cover tightly with a piece of buttered greaseproof paper. Cover this with foil and a tightly fitting lid. Bring to the boil, then reduce the heat and simmer very gently for 1½–2 hours, until the meat is tender, the liquid well absorbed and the stew rich and pulpy. Add the remaining parsley, taste and adjust the seasoning if necessary and serve with a glass of stout.

Cook's Tips
Broad shoulder chops or stewing lamb can also be used for Irish Stew. The carrots are not strictly traditional, but I feel they give a more tasty and interesting dish.

The cooking liquid could be half stock and half Irish dry stout, although again this is not truly traditional!

If the potatoes are waxy they will not break down and thicken the cooking liquid. In this case, thicken the liquid before serving by removing a few of the potato slices, mashing and stirring back into the stew.

Preparation time
20 minutes

Cooking time
1½–2 hours

Oven temperature
160°C (325°F), Gas Mark 3

160°C or 325°F. (= moderately slow.)

Serves 4

You will need
1 kg/2 lb neck of lamb, cut into rings about 1.5 cm/¾ inch thick
2 large onions, sliced
1 kg/2 lb floury potatoes, sliced
2 large carrots, sliced
2–3 tablespoons finely chopped parsley
400 ml/14 fl oz lamb stock or water
salt and pepper

Lambs' Liver with Bacon, Onions and Champ

Fry the bacon rashers in a little hot oil until brown and beginning to crisp. Remove from the pan and keep warm. Fry the onion in the same pan until soft and just beginning to brown, then remove and keep warm.

Put the seasoned flour in a large polythene bag and add the slices of liver, one at a time, to coat evenly in the flour, then shake off the excess flour.

Add a little extra oil to the pan and quickly fry the liver until brown on both sides and cooked to your liking. Divide the liver, bacon and onions between 2 serving plates and serve immediately, with Champ (see page 92).

Cook's Tips
Calf's liver can be used instead of lambs' liver.

To make gravy, add a little water to the sediment in the pan, stir well and bring to the boil for a few minutes, then strain and serve with the liver, bacon and onions.

Preparation time
10 minutes

Cooking time
10–15 minutes

Serves 2

You will need
4 rashers of bacon, rinded
vegetable oil for frying
1 large onion, sliced
2 tablespoons plain flour, seasoned
500 g/1 lb lambs' liver, sliced
salt and pepper

EXTRA STOUT
GUINNESS
SIMONS & CO.
BELFAST
ST JAMES'S GATE DUBLIN

Dublin Coddle

Layer the onions, bacon, sausages and potatoes in a large saucepan or flameproof casserole, sprinkling half the parsley between the layers and seasoning each layer with salt and pepper. Pour on the water or stock, bring to the boil, then press a sheet of greaseproof paper on top of the stew. Cover with a tightly fitting lid, reduce the heat and simmer for 1–1½ hours, until the liquid is greatly reduced and the potatoes are broken down and thickening the liquid. Taste and adjust the seasoning, stir in the remaining parsley and serve hot, with soda bread and a glass of stout.

Preparation time
15 minutes

Cooking time
1–1½ hours

Serves 4

You will need
3 large onions, sliced
8 slices of bacon, 5mm/¼ inch thick
5 large pork sausages, cut in chunks
1 kg/2 lb potatoes, sliced
4 tablespoons finely chopped parsley
300 ml/½ pint water or stock
salt and pepper

Pork Ribs and Onions

Wash the ribs and cut into similar-sized pieces. Put into a large saucepan and add the water or stock. Bring to the boil and skim. Add the onions, herbs and salt and pepper, cover, reduce the heat and simmer for 2–2½ hours, until the pork is tender and beginning to fall off the bones.

In a cup, blend the cornflour with a little of the cooking liquid, then stir back into the pan to thicken. Add the parsley, taste and adjust the seasoning and serve with boiled potatoes and a glass of stout.

Preparation time
5 minutes

Cooking time
2–2½ hours

Serves 4

You will need
1kg/2 lb spare ribs
500 ml/1 pint water or stock
2 large onions, sliced
1 bay leaf, 4–5 parsley stalks, 5 cm/2 inch piece of celery stick and 1 blade of mace, tied together
1 tablespoon cornflour
2 tablespoons finely chopped parsley
salt and pepper

Boiled Bacon and Cabbage

Put the bacon into a large saucepan, cover with fresh cold water and bring to the boil. Discard this water, rinse the ham, wash out the pan and begin again with fresh water, this time adding the onion, carrots, celery, leek, peppercorns and herbs. Bring to the boil, then cover the pan and simmer for 25 minutes per 500 g/1 lb.

Add the cabbage wedges 20–25 minutes before the end of the cooking time and continue to simmer until the meat and cabbage are tender.

Remove the bacon and cabbage from the cooking liquid and drain the cabbage. Peel the rind from the bacon and serve sliced, with the cabbage, boiled potatoes and parsley sauce, if liked.

Cook's Tip
A 2 kg/4 lb joint of bacon will give approximately 10–20 slices, plus a 150 g/5 oz tail piece which is ideal for Chicken and Ham Pie (see page 81).

Preparation time
10–15 minutes, plus soaking overnight

Cooking time
1 hour 40 minutes

Serves 6–8

You will need
2 kg/4 lb joint of bacon (green or smoked), tied in a neat shape and soaked overnight in cold water
1 onion, quartered
2 carrots, quartered
2 celery sticks, quartered
1 large leek, quartered
10 peppercorns
2 bay leaves, 1 sprig of thyme, 4–5 parsley stalks and 1 blade of mace, tied together
1 tight-headed green cabbage, cut into wedges, core removed

Roast Stuffed Pork Fillet

Melt half the butter in a frying pan and fry the onion until soft but not coloured. Stir in the breadcrumbs, lemon rind, herbs and salt and pepper to taste. Leave until cold. If necessary, bind with a little beaten egg.

Slit the pork fillets lengthways without cutting right through, then flatten by beating very lightly with a rolling pin. Spread the stuffing over one of the fillets, turning in the ends. Lay the second fillet on top, tuck in the ends and wrap the long sides around to encase the stuffing. Tie at intervals. Heat the remaining butter in a flameproof dish and brown the fillet on all sides. Pour in the boiling water, cover tightly and cook in a preheated oven at 180°C (350°F), Gas Mark 4 for 1–1¼ hours.

Remove the string and transfer the pork to a hot serving dish. Thicken the cooking juices with the arrowroot and stock mixture, taste and adjust the seasoning. Slice the pork and serve with the gravy, and apple sauce, if liked.

Cook's Tips
Soaked prunes, stones removed and flesh chopped, make an interesting addition to the stuffing.

Take care not to overcook the pork, or it will become tough and stringy.

Preparation time
30 minutes

Cooking time
1–1¼ hours

Oven temperature
180°C (350°F), Gas Mark 4

Serves 4

You will need
1 large onion, finely chopped
50 g/2 oz butter
175 g/6 oz fresh white breadcrumbs
grated rind of ½ lemon
pinch of dried thyme
1½ tablespoons finely chopped parsley
a little beaten egg, to bind (optional)
2 pork fillets, about 375 g/12 oz each
150 ml/¼ pint boiling water
1 tablespoon arrowroot, blended with 300 ml/½ pint stock
salt and pepper

Roasted Pig's Trotters

Put the trotters, onions, carrots, herbs and peppercorns in a large saucepan, cover with water and bring to the boil. Cover and simmer for 2–3 hours, until the meat is tender. Remove the trotters from the cooking liquid, drain and pat dry with absorbent kitchen paper. Dip in beaten egg and roll in the breadcrumbs.

Heat some bacon fat or oil in a shallow roasting dish, lay the crumbed trotters in the dish and spoon over the hot fat. Roast in a preheated oven at 220°C (425°F), Gas Mark 7 for 15–30 minutes, until crisp and golden. Serve with Soda Bread (see pages 114–115) and a glass of stout.

Cook's Tip
Pig's knees are another delicacy in Ireland, prepared in exactly the same way as the feet. They are slightly more substantial as there is more meat on them. Serve with a mustard sauce, boiled cabbage and Pickled Beetroot (see page 93).

Preparation time
10 minutes

Cooking time
Boiling: 2–3 hours
Roasting: 15–30 minutes

Oven temperature
220°C (425°F), Gas Mark 7

Serves 4

You will need
4 pig's feet, well washed
2 large onions, halved
2 large carrots, halved
2 bay leaves, 8–10 parsley stalks, 1 sprig of thyme, tied together
12 peppercorns
1 egg (size 4), beaten
125 g/4 oz dried breadcrumbs (Cook's Tip, page 66)
bacon fat or oil for roasting
bunch of parsley, to garnish

Chickens were once regarded as a luxury. Although the poorest country families would have kept a few hens, it was for their eggs rather than their flesh. Today, however, poultry is the most widely used of all meats. Game remains the preserve of the country sportsman and the more adventurous cook. Many of the old recipes are still in use.

Poultry and Game

Pot Roast Chicken with Parsley Stuffing

Fry the onion in 50 g/2 oz of the melted butter until soft, stir in the breadcrumbs, herbs and salt and pepper to taste. Bind with the beaten egg. Leave until cold.

Stuff the chicken breast and body cavity, then truss. Fry the bacon and button onions in the oil until browned. Transfer to a large saucepan or flameproof casserole. Brown the chicken all over in the remaining fat. Put the chicken on top of the onions and bacon, and add the carrots, turnip, bouquet garni and stock. Bring to the boil, cover and simmer for 1¼–1½ hours, until the chicken is cooked. Transfer the chicken to a large serving dish; surround with the vegetables. Keep warm while making the sauce.

Blend the remaining butter with the flour until smooth, then gradually whisk into the boiling cooking liquid until it thickens. Season to taste, strain and serve with the chicken.

Preparation time
30 minutes

Cooking time
1¼–1½ hours

Oven temperature
180°C (350°F), Gas Mark 4

Serves 4–6

You will need

1 large onion, finely chopped
65 g/2½oz butter
125–150 g/4–5 oz fine fresh white breadcrumbs
3 tablespoons finely chopped parsley
pinch of dried mixed herbs
1 small egg, beaten
1.75–2.25 kg/3½–4½ lb roasting chicken
250 g/8 oz bacon, in one piece, rinded and cut into large cubes
12 button onions, peeled
2 tablespoons vegetable oil
500 g/1 lb carrots, cut in chunks
250 g/8 oz turnip, cut in chunks
1 bouquet garni (Cook's Tip, page 10)
450 ml/¾ pint strong chicken stock
1 tablespoon plain flour
salt and pepper

Frigasse of Chicken

Melt the butter, stir in the flour and gradually add the liquid to make a smooth sauce; cook for a few minutes. Blend the egg yolk with the cream and whisk into the sauce with the Worcestershire sauce, mustard, anchovy sauce, capers, parsley and salt and pepper to taste. Fold in the chicken pieces, mushrooms and onions and heat thoroughly. Serve on a large flat dish, garnished with the bacon rolls, lemon wedges, watercress and a dusting of paprika pepper.

Cook's Tip
Frigasse or fricassée is a word used to describe a method of cooking poultry, lamb, veal, rabbit, fish or vegetables by boiling or stewing in stock or milk. This liquid is then thickened with egg yolks and cream.

Preparation time
30 minutes

Cooking time
15–30 minutes

Serves 4–6

You will need

50 g/2 oz butter
50 g/2 oz plain flour
300 ml/½ pint chicken stock
300 ml/½ pint milk
1 egg yolk
65 ml/2½ fl oz double cream
1–2 tablespoons Worcestershire sauce
1 tablespoon mustard
1 teaspoon anchovy sauce
2 teaspoons capers
2 tablespoons finely chopped parsley
750 g/1½ lb cooked chicken breast cut into large strips
175 g/6 oz button mushrooms, fried
16 pickling onions, skinned and boiled
salt and pepper

To garnish

8 rashers of bacon, cut in half, rolled and grilled
4 lemon wedges
bunch of watercress
paprika

Boned Stuffed Chicken

Fry the onion in half the butter until soft but not coloured, stir in the breadcrumbs, herbs and salt and pepper to taste. Bind with the beaten egg. Leave until cold.

Lay the boned chicken in front of you, skin side down, pull the wings and legs through to the inside and flatten the bird. Lay the slices of ham over the breast meat and spread the sausage meat over the ham. Lay a log of the stuffing down the centre of the bird. Fold over the sides of the chicken, tucking in excess flesh and skin at the neck and tail. Do not stretch the skin, otherwise it will burst during cooking. Stitch the edges together.

Place in a roasting pan, breast side up. Rub with the remaining butter, pour on the stock and cook in a preheated oven at 190°C (375°F), Gas Mark 5 for about 2 hours, until cooked through. Serve hot or cold, cut in slices.

Cook's Tip
The breadcrumb stuffing can be varied by adding chopped mushrooms, walnuts and mushroom ketchup, and by placing 1–2 hard boiled eggs in the centre of the stuffing, which looks attractive when sliced.

Preparation time
30–40 minutes

Cooking time
2 hours

Oven temperature
190°C (375°F), Gas Mark 5

Serves 12–20

You will need
1 large onion, finely chopped
125 g/4 oz butter
250 g/8 oz fine fresh white breadcrumbs
1 tablespoon finely chopped parsley
1 tablespoon finely chopped chervil
1 tablespoon finely chopped tarragon
1 egg, beaten
2–2.5 kg/4–5 lb roasting chicken, boned. with the skin unpunctured
2 large slices of uncooked ham or bacon, cut 3 mm/⅛ inch thick, rinded
375 g/12 oz pork sausage meat
300 ml/½ pint hot chicken stock
salt and pepper

Pheasant with Mustard Sauce

Heat the butter in a large frying pan and cook the pheasant breasts, skin side down, over a gentle heat for 3–4 minutes. Turn and cook the other side for a further 3–4 minutes. Remove from the heat, season with salt and pepper and leave to rest for 3 minutes before serving.

To make the sauce, put the stock, wine and port in a saucepan and boil to reduce by half. Stir in the mustard and cream and reduce until the sauce thickens and coats the back of a spoon. Season to taste.

Boil the cabbage until just cooked; drain, toss in the butter and season to taste. Divide between 4 warmed serving plates, piling it in the centre. Carve each pheasant breast into 3 slices and arrange in a fan on top of the cabbage. Spoon a little of the sauce over each breast. Serve with Champ (see page 92).

Cook's Tip
Cooking times will depend on the thickness of the pheasant breast. When cooked the flesh should feel firm but springy to the touch.

Preparation time
10 minutes

Cooking time
6–8 minutes

Serves 4

You will need
4–6 tablespoons clarified butter (Cook's Tip, page 53)
4 pheasant breasts, about 100–150 g/3½–5 oz, skin and wing bones removed
salt and pepper

Mustard sauce
300 ml/½ pint game stock (Cook's Tip, page 21)
300 ml/½ pint red wine
2 tablespoons port
2-4 tablespoons coarse grain mustard
300 ml/½ pint single cream

To serve
425 g/14 oz Savoy cabbage, shredded
50 g/2 oz butter

Roast Breast of Chicken with Oatmeal Stuffing

Put the wine in a saucepan, bring to the boil and reduce by half. Add the chicken stock and boil to reduce by half again.

Meanwhile make the stuffing. Fry the onion in half the butter, stir in the oatmeal, parsley and seasoning. Leave until cold. Lay the breasts skin side down, fold back the piece of fillet meat on the underside of the breast. Cut a pocket about 4 cm/1½ inches long in the flesh opposite the fillet; take care not to cut completely through the breast. Divide the stuffing into 4 and place in the pockets. Fold over the flap of meat to enclose the stuffing.

Brown the breasts on both sides in the remaining butter. Transfer to a baking sheet and roast in a preheated oven at 230°C (450°F), Gas Mark 8, until cooked. Serve on a bed of Roasted Root Vegetables (see page 89) with the sauce, caramelized onions (Cook's Tip) and Champ (see page 92).

Cook's Tip
To caramelize onions, cook 20 peeled pickling onions in boiling water until almost tender, drain and fry gently in 25 g/1 oz butter and 1 teaspoon sugar in a covered pan, shaking continually until the onions are an even golden brown.

Preparation time
30 minutes

Cooking time
20–30 minutes

Oven temperature
230°C (450°F), Gas Mark 8

Serves 4

You will need
300 ml/½ pint red wine
900 ml/1½ pints strong chicken stock
1 onion, finely chopped
125 g/4 oz butter
75 g/3 oz coarse oatmeal
3 tablespoons finely chopped parsley
4 chicken breasts, about 175–200 g/6–7 oz each,skin and small wing bone left on
salt and pepper

Roast Goose with Apple and Whiskey Stuffing

Truss the goose, prick all over and set on a wire rack in a roasting tin. Season with salt and pepper. Place in a preheated oven at 240°C (475°F) Gas Mark 9 for 30 minutes, then reduce the heat to 190°C (375°F) Gas Mark 5 for a further 3½–4½ hours, allowing a total cooking time of 20–25 minutes per 500 g/1 lb. Pour off the fat several times during the cooking; reserve for future use.

Soak the grated apple in the whiskey. Fry the onion in the butter until soft, then add the soaked apple, breadcrumbs, herbs, lemon rind and seasoning. Bind with the egg. Grease a 900 ml/1½ pint ovenproof soufflé dish with goose fat and fill with the stuffing. Cover and cook with the goose for 45 minutes. Some of the stuffing can be used to fill the cavity of small, cored Cox's apples which can be baked for 30 minutes with the goose. Leave the goose to rest in a warm place for 15–20 minutes before carving. Serve with gravy, roast potatoes and Braised Red Cabbage (see page 88).

Cook's Tip
The reserved goose fat is excellent for roasting potatoes and parsnips and for greasing baking tins. It will keep in the refrigerator for months.

Preparation time
30 minutes

Cooking time
4–5 hours

Oven temperature
240°C (475°F), Gas Mark 9, then 190°C (375°F), Gas Mark 5

Serves 6

You will need
6 kg/12 lb goose, oven-ready, with giblets to make stock for the gravy
1 Cox's apple, peeled, cored and grated
2 tablespoons malt whiskey
1 onion, finely chopped
25 g/1 oz butter
250 g/8 oz coarse fresh white breadcrumbs
2 tablespoons finely chopped parsley
1 tablespoon finely chopped sage
pinch of grated lemon rind
1 egg (size 4), beaten
salt and pepper

Roast Pheasant

Use the pheasant giblets to make the gravy. Fry the giblets in half the butter with the onion, celery and carrot, until browned. Pour on the red wine and boil fiercely to reduce by half. Add the water, bay leaf and peppercorns, then simmer while preparing and roasting the pheasant.

Smear the pheasant with the remaining butter, season with salt and pepper, set in a roasting dish and cook for 20–25 minutes per 500 g/1 lb in a preheated oven at 220°C (425°F), Gas Mark 7, basting several times during the cooking. Once the bird is cooked, cover loosely and leave to rest for 10 minutes before carving.

Meanwhile, strain the stock and boil quickly to reduce to 200 ml/7 fl oz. Drain all but 1 tablespoon of fat from the roasting dish, add the flour and stir well to mix with the sediment. Blend in the stock, bring to the boil, stirring frequently, then strain. Serve the pheasant, garnished with watercress and accompanied by the gravy, brussels sprouts, root vegetables, roast potatoes and game chips.

Cook's Tip
Since pheasant is a lean meat with a fine skin it is important to smear it well with butter or oil and to baste it several times while roasting. It can also be covered with rashers of fat bacon to protect it from drying out during the cooking.

Preparation time
20 minutes

Cooking time
35–45 minutes

Cooking temperature
220°C (425°F), Gas Mark 7

Serves 2

You will need
1 plump pheasant, about 875 g/1¾ lb, oven-ready, with giblets (heart, gizzard and neck), washed
50 g/2 oz butter
1 small onion, quartered
1 celery stick, chopped
1 small carrot, sliced
65 ml/2½ fl oz red wine
450 ml/¾ pint water
1 bay leaf
6 peppercorns
2 tablespoons plain flour
salt and pepper
watercress, to garnish

Chicken and Ham Pie

Melt 50 g/2 oz of the butter in a large saucepan, stir in the flour, cook for a few minutes, then gradually add the stock and milk to make a thick sauce. Season to taste with the mustard, mace, parsley, salt and pepper. Fry the onion and mushrooms in the remaining butter until cooked, then stir into the sauce with the chicken and ham. Leave until cold.

Roll out the pastry and cut a long strip about 1 cm/½ inch wide to go around the rim of a 25 cm/10 inch enamel pie plate. Use half the pastry to line the plate and add the pastry strip to give a double edge. Pile the filling in the centre and brush the pastry edge with beaten egg. Use the remaining pastry to make a lid for the pie and seal well, fluting the edges.

Decorate with the pastry trimmings, brush with egg and place in a preheated oven at 220°C (425°F0, Gas Mark 7 for 25–30 minutes, until golden brown. Serve with boiled or baked potatoes and green vegetables or salad.

Cook's Tip
This is very much a traditional pie and is an excellent way to use up leftover cooked chicken and ham. Mixed vegetables can also be included in the sauce.

Preparation time
30 minutes

Cooking time
25–30 minutes

Oven temperature
220°C (425°F), Gas Mark 7

Serves 6–8

You will need
- 75 g/3 oz butter
- 50 g/2 oz plain flour
- 175 ml/6 fl oz chicken stock
- 150 ml/¼ pint milk
- 1 teaspoon English mustard
- pinch of ground mace
- 1 tablespoon finely chopped parsley
- 1 small onion, finely chopped
- 175 g/6 oz mushrooms, sliced
- 375–500 g/¾–1 lb cooked chicken, cut into bite-sized pieces
- 175 g/6 oz cooked ham, cut into bite-sized pieces
- 500 g/1 lb puff or flaky pastry, thawed if frozen
- 1 egg (size 4), beaten
- salt and pepper

Pheasant and Rabbit Stew with Bacon

Toss all the meat in the flour and fry in batches in the hot oil until browned all over. Transfer to a flameproof casserole along with any remaining flour. Fry the bacon until it begins to colour, then fry the onions. Add to the casserole along with the wine, stock, herbs and seasoning. Bring to the boil, then reduce the heat and simmer for 1–1½ hours, until the meat is tender. Remove the herbs, taste and adjust the seasoning, stir in the parsley and garnish with triangles of fried bread.

Cook's Tips
250 g/8 oz button mushrooms can be added with the onions; Guinness or all pheasant stock can be used instead of wine.

When frying meat, it is important not to put it in the pan all at once, otherwise it will stew rather than fry and will not brown successfully; the flavour and colour of the finished dish will therefore not be as good.

Preparation time
30 minutes

Cooking time
1–1½ hours

Oven temperature
180°C (350°F), Gas Mark 4

Serves 4–6

You will need
4 pheasant legs, skinned, boned and cubed
1 large rabbit, skinned, boned and cubed
2 tablespoons plain flour
2 tablespoons oil
175 g/6 oz bacon in one piece trimmed and cubed
16 pickling onions, peeled
250 ml/8 fl oz red wine
250 ml/8 fl oz pheasant stock
1 bay leaf, 1 sprig of thyme, 1 blade of mace and 4–5 parsley stalks, tied together
salt and pepper

To garnish
2 tablespoons finely chopped parsley
triangles of fried bread

Rabbit Casserole with Prunes and Herbs

Put the rabbit pieces in a large glass bowl with the wine, vinegar, onion, carrot and herbs. Leave to marinade for 24 hours in the refrigerator.

Remove the rabbit from the marinade, pat dry on kitchen paper and fry in hot oil and butter until browned.
Transfer the rabbit to a large saucepan or flameproof casserole and add the marinade, game stock, mustard and seasoning. Bring to the boil, then reduce the heat and simmer gently for 1–2 hours, until tender.

Transfer the rabbit pieces to a serving dish. Push the vegetables and cooking liquid through a sieve into a clean pan, bring to the boil, stir in the cream and prunes and taste and adjust the seasoning. Pour over the rabbit, sprinkle with parsley and serve with boiled floury potatoes.

Cook's Tip
To joint a rabbit, remove the ribs, shoulder and neck, cutting from the body just below the ribs. Use to make stock. Divide the saddle and legs just above the top of the legs, remove the membrane and flap, cut the saddle and legs in half.

Preparation time
30 minutes, plus overnight marinating

Cooking time
1–2 hours

Serves 4

You will need
1 large rabbit, skinned and jointed (Cook's Tip)
150 ml/¼ pint red wine
1 teaspoon vinegar
175 g/6 oz onion, coarsely chopped
175 g/6 oz carrot, coarsely chopped
1 bay leaf, 4–5 parsley stalks and 1sprig of thyme, tied together
1 tablespoon vegetable oil
25 g/1 oz butter
450 ml/¾ pint game stock (Cook's Tip, page 21)
1 teaspoon coarse grain mustard
65 ml/2½ fl oz double cream
175 g/6 oz prunes, soaked overnight in boiling tea
2 tablespoons finely chopped parsley
salt and pepper

Rabbit Frigasse

Joint the rabbit (Cook's Tip, above), then place in a large bowl and cover with water; add a little salt and vinegar. Leave to soak overnight to whiten and tenderize the flesh.

Discard the soaking water, put the rabbit in a saucepan and cover with fresh water; bring to the boil. Discard this water and add the stock, milk, onions and herbs and simmer for 1–2 hours, until tender.

Melt the butter in a large saucepan, stir in the flour and gradually add 600 ml/1 pint of the cooking liquid, stirring continually over a gentle heat to make a smooth thick sauce. Stir in the cream and mustard, taste and adjust the seasoning. Add the rabbit pieces and the fried mushrooms. Heat thoroughly, then serve hot, garnished with parsley.

Cook's Tips
Rabbit bred for the table will take much less time to cook than wild rabbit and your butcher will prepare it for you.

The sauce can also be garnished with fried button onions and grilled bacon rolls as for Chicken Frigasse (see page 74).

Preparation time
30 minutes, plus overnight soaking

Cooking time
1–2 hours

Serves 4

You will need
1 or 2 rabbits, to give approximately 1.75 kg/3½ lb when prepared
600 ml/1 pint chicken stock
300 ml/½ pint milk
2 large onions, thinly sliced
1 bay leaf, 1 sprig of thyme and 4–5 parsley stalks, tied together
50 g/2 oz butter
50 g/2 oz plain flour
150 ml/¼ pint cream
1 teaspoon mustard
175 g/6 oz button mushrooms, fried in butter
salt and pepper
2 tablespoons finely chopped parsley, to garnish

Potted Goose with Juniper Berries

Shred the goose meat finely, using 2 forks to pull it apart. Alternatively the meat can be roughly chopped in a food processor, but this will create a different texture. It should not be overprocessed, otherwise it will become too smooth.

Mix the shredded meat with the juniper berries, nutmeg, sage, salt and pepper and about two-thirds of the goose fat. Pack into individual pots or ramekin dishes or 1 large container. Pour the remaining fat on top to seal the surface of the meat.

Serve in the pots or spoon on to individual serving dishes. Garnish with salad leaves and accompany by hot toast or Irish Wheaten Bread (see page 115).

Cook's Tip
Leftover meat from roast game such as venison, pheasant or rabbit can be prepared in the same way, using unsalted butter instead of the goose fat for potting, and clarified butter (Cook's Tip, page 53) for sealing.

Preparation time
15 minutes

Serves 4

You will need
300 g/10 oz freshly cooked goose meat
24 juniper berries, crushed
pinch of grated nutmeg
3 teaspoons finely chopped fresh sage
75 g/3 oz goose fat, melted
salt and pepper
salad leaves, to garnish
hot toast, to serve

Venison Stew with Parsnip and Potato Champ

Heat half the oil in a large frying pan and fry the onion until soft and beginning to brown. Transfer to a large saucepan or flameproof casserole. Fry the venison in batches in the remaining oil until brown. Add to the pan with the onion. Stir in the flour, then add the Guinness and stock or water, the bay leaf, marjoram and salt and pepper. Bring to the boil, then reduce the heat and simmer gently for 1–1½ hours, until the meat is almost tender. Alternatively the stew can be cooked in a preheated oven at 150–160°C (300–325°F), Gas Mark 2–3.

Add the onions and celery 15–30 minutes before the end of the cooking time. Taste and adjust the seasoning, stir in the parsley and serve with parsnip champ.

Cook's Tip
To make parsnip champ, allow 1 kg/1 lb potatoes and 1 kg/1 lb parsnips for 4 servings. Cook the vegetables separately until tender, drain and dry well, then mash together with plenty of butter and seasoning.

Preparation time
15 minutes

Cooking time
1½–2 hours

Oven temperature
150–160°C (300–325°F), Gas Mark 2–3

Serves 4–6

You will need
1–2 tablespoons vegetable oil
1 onion, finely chopped
750 g–1 kg/1½–2 lb lean venison meat, off the bone, cut into 2.5 cm/1 inch cubes
25 g/1 oz plain flour
300 ml/½ pint Guinness
750 ml/1¼ pints game stock or water
1 bay leaf
1 sprig of fresh marjoram
12–18 pickling onions, peeled
125–175 g/4–6 oz celery, cut into 2.5 cm/1 inch lengths
2 tablespoons finely chopped parsley
salt and pepper
parsnip champ, to serve (Cook's Tip)

Cultivated vegetables – particularly root vegetables such as potatoes, parsnips, carrots and onions, along with cabbage – have been fundamental to the dishes of Ireland, a largely agricultural country. The potato became the staple food in the seventeenth and eighteenth centuries. Today, vegetables form the basis of many soups and stews as well as making colourful accompaniments to other dishes.

Vegetable Dishes

Parsnip Cakes

Put the parsnips, flour, mace, nutmeg, salt, pepper and butter into a large bowl and beat well to combine. Divide into 4 pieces and shape each piece into a round flat cake about 9 cm/ 3½ inches in diameter and 1–1.5 cm/½–¾ inch deep. Cut each cake into a half-moon shape.

Dip each cake into the beaten egg, then into the breadcrumbs, pressing them well into the cakes to give an even coating. Fry the cakes in a little hot oil for 3–4 minutes on each side, until cooked through and an even golden colour. Drain on absorbent kitchen paper and serve as a main course or side dish. Parsnip cakes are particularly good with pork, ham and roast beef, or with fried sausages and bacon.

Cook's Tip
Any vegetable suitable for mashing, such as carrots, potatoes or turnips, can be used for this recipe, either on their own or in a combination of 2 or more. Different spices and herbs can be added to give variety. The cakes can also be shaped into small logs or croquettes and deep-fried.

Preparation time
20–30 minutes

Cooking time
6–8 minutes

Makes 8 cakes

You will need
500 g/1 lb parsnips, cooked and mashed
6 tablespoons plain flour
pinch of ground mace
pinch of ground nutmeg
5 g/¼ oz butter, melted
1 egg (size 2), beaten
125–175 g/4–6 oz fresh breadcrumbs
vegetable oil for shallow frying
salt and pepper

Braised Sweet and Sour Red Cabbage

In a large ovenproof casserole combine the cabbage, onion, garlic, apples, sugar, spices, grated ginger, salt and pepper. Mix the vinegar with the stock or water and pour over the cabbage. Dot with the butter, then cover closely with greaseproof paper and a tightly fitting lid. Bring to the boil, then reduce the heat and simmer for 1–1½ hours, until the vegetables are tender.

Alternatively the casserole can be transferred to a preheated oven at 160°C (325°F), Gas Mark 3 after the liquid has been brought to the boil. Stir once or twice during the cooking time. This is traditionally served with goose, duck, game and pork.

Cook's Tips
This is an excellent dish to prepare in large quantities, since it both freezes and reheats well.

Hard, white drumhead cabbage can be used instead of the red cabbage, but the colour is less inviting.

Preparation time
15 minutes

Cooking time
1–1½ hours

Oven temperature
160°C (325°F), Gas Mark 3

Serves 6–8

You will need
500 g/1 lb red cabbage, quartered, cored and very thinly sliced
1 onion, sliced
1 garlic clove, finely chopped
375 g/12 oz cooking apples, peeled, cored and sliced
2 tablespoons demerara sugar
pinch each of ground mace, nutmeg and cinnamon
¼ teaspoon ground allspice
¼ teaspoon grated fresh root ginger
2 tablespoons red wine vinegar
150 ml/¼ pint vegetable stock or water
50 g/2 oz butter
salt and pepper

Mushroom Frigasse

Heat 50 g/2 oz of the butter in a large frying pan and fry the onion and garlic until soft but not coloured. Add the prepared mushrooms and continue to cook over a gentle heat for about 10 minutes to draw out their juices; they should stew rather than fry. Add the marjoram, parsley, salt and pepper and red wine and bring to the boil.

Remove the frying pan from the heat. Blend the egg yolk with the cornflour and cream and stir into the wine and mushroom juices to thicken. Keep warm.

Toast the bread and cut 3 circles from each slice, using a 9 cm/ 3½ inch cutter. Lay the circles of hot toast overlapping on individual serving plates and pile the frigasse on to the toast. Sprinkle with parsley and serve immediately.

Cook's Tips
Cultivated or wild mushrooms can be used for this dish; use just one type or a mixture of varieties.

The frigasse is also delicious with small strips of fried bacon stirred in just before serving.

Preparation time
15–20 minutes

Cooking time
20–25 minutes

Serves 4 as a main course, 8 as a first course

You will need
75 g/3 oz butter
1 onion, finely chopped
1 garlic clove, crushed
875 g/1¾ lb mushrooms of your choice, cleaned and sliced if large
1 teaspoon finely chopped marjoram
1 tablespoon finely chopped parsley
150 ml/¼ pint red wine
1 egg yolk
1 teaspoon cornflour
2 tablespoons single cream
salt and pepper

To serve
9 slices of bread
2 tablespoons finely chopped parsley

Roasted Root Vegetables

Cut the prepared vegetables into 1 cm/½ inch cubes and fry quickly in the oil until just coloured. Transfer to a roasting dish, drizzle on the honey, toss to coat evenly and roast in a preheated oven at 200°C (400°F), Gas Mark 6 for 1–1¼ hours, until tender and well glazed.

Toss frequently during cooking to prevent the honey from burning. Serve with roasted meat, poultry and game.

Preparation time
15 minutes

Cooking time
1–1¼ hours

Oven temperature
200°C (400°F), Gas Mark 6

Serves 6

You will need
500 g/1 lb carrots, peeled
500 g/1 lb parsnips, peeled
500 g/1 lb turnips, peeled
1 tablespoon vegetable oil
2 tablespoons honey

Vegetable Stew with Herb Dumplings

Heat the oil in a large flameproof casserole and fry the onion until soft. Cut the carrots, celery, turnip and potatoes into large (approximately 2.5 cm/1 inch) chunks and add to the onion. Cover closely with greaseproof paper and sweat over a gentle heat for 5 minutes. Add the tomatoes, stock, tomato purée, paprika, salt, pepper and half the parsley. Bring to the boil, then simmer gently for 15–20 minutes.

Meanwhile, prepare the dumplings. Rub the butter into the flour until it resembles fine breadcrumbs. Add the herbs and salt and pepper and mix with the egg and enough water to form a sticky dough. Using a wet spoon, drop 8 tablespoons of the dough on to the simmering stew. Cover and cook for 20–30 minutes, until the vegetables are tender. Serve hot, garnished with the remaining parsley.

Cook's Tips
Any combination of vegetables, herbs and seasonings can be used for this stew.

The dumplings can be replaced with a topping of Savoury Scones (see page 118), in which case the stew should be cooked in a preheated oven at 220°C (425°F), Gas Mark 7 for 25 minutes.

Preparation time
20–30 minutes

Cooking time
30–40 minutes

Serves 4

You will need
2 tablespoons vegetable oil
1 large onion, sliced
2 large carrots (about 400 g/13 oz)
3–4 celery sticks (about 300 g/10 oz)
175 g/6 oz turnip, peeled
500 g/1 lb potatoes
425 g/14 oz canned plum tomatoes
750 ml/1¼ pints vegetable stock
1 tablespoon tomato purée
1 teaspoon paprika
4 tablespoons chopped parsley
salt and pepper

Dumplings
50 g/2 oz butter
125 g/4 oz self-raising flour
2 tablespoons chopped parsley
1 teaspoon chopped thyme or marjoram
1 small egg (size 4), beaten

Champ

Wash the potatoes and boil in their skins in salted water until tender. Drain and return to the pan to dry over a low heat, covered with a piece of absorbent kitchen paper. Peel the potatoes and mash well.

While the potatoes are cooking, put the milk and chopped spring onions into a saucepan, bring to the boil and simmer for a few minutes. Gradually beat the milk into the mashed potatoes to form a soft but not sloppy mixture. Beat in half the butter, season to taste with salt and pepper and divide between 4 warmed plates or bowls. Make a hollow in the centre of the mixture in each bowl, cut the remaining butter into 4 pieces and put one in each hollow; serve immediately.

Cook's Tips
Champ is one of the most famous Irish dishes and traditionally would have been served as a main meal with a glass of milk or buttermilk. Nowadays it is used as an accompaniment to meats such as boiled ham and grilled sausages.

Parsley, young nettle tops, peas and broad beans can be substituted for the spring onions.

Preparation time
5 minutes

Cooking time
20–25 minutes

Serves 4

You will need
1 kg/2 lb potatoes
150 ml/¼ pint milk
4–5 spring onions, finely chopped
50–125 g/2–4 oz butter
salt and pepper

Colcannon

Cook the kale or cabbage in boiling water for 10–20 minutes, until very tender. Boil the potatoes in their skins until tender. Simmer the spring onions or chives in the milk or cream for about 5 minutes.

Drain the cabbage and mash. Drain the potatoes, peel and mash well; add the hot milk and spring onions, beating well to give a soft fluffy texture. Beat in the kale or cabbage, with salt, pepper and half the butter to give a speckled green colour. Heat through thoroughly before serving in individual dishes or bowls. Make a well in the centre of the colcannon and put a knob of the remaining butter in each; serve immediately.

Colcannon, like champ, can be served as a main dish with a glass of buttermilk or as an accompanying vegetable.

Cook's Tip
Sometimes I blend the kale or cabbage in a food processor together with the hot milk and spring onions before adding them to the mashed potatoes. This produces Colcannon with an even texture and overall green colour.

Preparation time
15 minutes

Cooking time
20 minutes

Serves 4–6

You will need
500 g/1 lb kale or green leaf cabbage, stalks removed, finely shredded
500 g/1 lb potatoes
6 spring onions or chives, finely chopped
150 ml/¼ pint milk or single cream
125 g/4 oz butter
salt and pepper

Pickled Beetroot

Put the beetroot in a large saucepan, and use a measuring jug to add water to cover. Add the salt, allowing 15 g/½ oz for every 600 ml/1 pint of water. Boil for 1½–2 hours, until tender.

While the beetroot is cooking prepare the spiced vinegar. Bruise the spices in a mortar and pestle, or place between 2 sheets of greaseproof paper and crush lightly with a weight. Tie the spices in a piece of muslin and place in a pan with the vinegar. Bring to the boil, then cover with a tightly fitting lid, remove from the heat and leave to infuse for 2 hours.

When the beetroot is cooked, leave until cool enough to handle, then peel and slice or cube the beetroot and pack loosely into sterilized preserving jars. Cover with the cold spiced vinegar and seal. Serve the pickled beetroot with hot or cold meat and game.

Cook's Tip
The spiced vinegar can also be used to pickle cauliflower florets, onions, mushrooms and red cabbage. I add a few extra spices to the jars for storage and presentation.

Preparation time
15 minutes, plus 2 hours infusing

Cooking time
1½–2 hours

Makes 4 x 600 ml/ 1 pint jars

You will need
1.5 kg/3 lb beetroot, washed and trimmed
approximately 1.8 litres/3 pints water
approximately 40 g/1½ oz salt

Spiced vinegar
5 cm/2 inch piece cinnamon stick
1 teaspoon whole cloves
1 teaspoon whole allspice
1 teaspoon whole black peppercorns
4 blades of mace
1.2 litres/2 pints distilled vinegar

Honey Pickled Vegetables

Place the vinegar, white wine, honey and spices in a large saucepan, bring to the boil and simmer for 5 minutes. Transfer to a large glass bowl and leave until cold.

Plunge the prepared vegetables into a large pan of boiling water, return to the boil, then drain and refresh under cold water until completely cold. Pack the vegetables into sterilized preserving jars, pour in the honey pickle, seal and leave for at least 3 days. Serve with rich meats and pâtés.

Cook's Tip
Miniature vegetables are perfect for pickling and look most attractive when served. Other spices such as mustard seeds, cardamom pods and coriander seeds can also be used.

Preparation time
20 minutes

Cooking time
10 minutes

You will need
900 ml/1½ pints white wine vinegar
300 ml/½ pint dry white wine
5 tablespoons honey
5 cm/2 inch piece cinnamon stick
8 allspice berries
12 whole black peppercorns
8 cloves
1.5 kg/3 lb mixed vegetables, such as cauliflower, broccoli, pickling onions, baby sweetcorn and carrots, prepared in even-sized pieces

In Ireland no meal is complete without the pudding or dessert. In addition to the traditional puddings such as apple tart there are many others introduced by both settlers and visitors. Using wild and cultivated fruits and grains, milk and eggs to make a rich range of mousses, fools, moulds and custards, there is indeed something for every occasion.

Puddings and Desserts

Carrageen Moss Blancmange

Put the carrageen moss, lemon rind and milk into a saucepan and slowly bring to the boil. Simmer gently for 15–20 minutes, until the carrageen swells and exudes jelly. Using a wooden spoon, beat the egg yolk and caster sugar together until pale, then pour on the carrageen mixture, stirring well.

Rub all the mixture through a strainer into a clean saucepan, bring to the boil and cook over a gentle heat, stirring constantly with a wooden spoon, until the mixture coats the back of the spoon. Leave until cold.

Whisk the egg white until stiff and gently fold into the cold carrageen mixture. Pour into a 900 ml/1½ pint wetted mould or 6 x 150 ml/¼ pint individual moulds or dishes. Refrigerate until set. Turn out of the mould and serve chilled, with lightly stewed fruit, fresh berry fruits or fruit purée.

Cook's Tip

Carrageen is an edible seaweed also known as Irish moss or sea moss. It is the vegetarian alternative to gelatine and is used for thickening both sweet and savoury dishes. It is available from health food and other specialist shops.

Preparation time
10 minutes, plus cooling and setting time

Cooking time
20–25 minutes

Serves 4–6

You will need

40 g/1½ oz dried carrageen moss
finely grated rind of 1 lemon
900 ml/1½ pints milk
1 egg (size 2), separated
2–3 tablespoons caster sugar

Irish Curd Cheesecake

Roll out the pastry no more than 3 mm/⅛ inch thick and use to line a 20 cm/8 inch loose-bottomed quiche tin. Place the tin on a baking sheet.

Cream the butter and sugar together until light and fluffy, then beat in the lemon rind and juice, cinnamon, egg yolks, flour and sieved cottage cheese. Beat the egg whites until stiff and fold into the mixture. Pour into the pastry case.

Combine all the ingredients for the topping and pour on top of the filling. Place in a preheated oven at 160°C (325°F), Gas Mark 3 for 1–1¼ hours, until the cake is golden in colour, risen and firm to the touch. Leave to cool in the tin. To serve, remove from the tin, sprinkle with icing sugar and serve with cream or yogurt.

Cook's Tip
This was a very popular dessert in Ireland during the eighteenth century, often flavoured with sherry, a favoured drink of the time. Sometimes the filling would have been varied by the addition of a few drops of rosewater or 50–125 g/2–4 oz dried fruit.

Preparation time
30 minutes

Cooking time
1–1¼ hours

Oven temperature
160°C (325°F), Gas Mark 3

Serves 6–8

You will need
125 g/4 oz Rich Shortcrust Pastry (see page 107)

Curd filling
50 g/2 oz butter, softened
50 g/2 oz caster sugar
rind of 1 large lemon
juice of ½ lemon
pinch of ground cinnamon
3 eggs (size 2), separated
3 tablespoons plain flour
375 g/12 oz cottage cheese, sieved

Topping
1 egg (size 2)
1 tablespoon caster sugar
25 g/1 oz butter, melted
1 tablespoon plain flour

Gooseberry and Elderflower Fool

Put the gooseberries, water and elderflower sprigs into a saucepan and simmer gently until the gooseberries are soft. Remove the elderflowers and turn the fruit into a sieve to drain off the excess juice. Put the gooseberries into a bowl and beat with a fork to form a purée. Sweeten the purée with sugar to taste and leave to cool.

Gently fold the whipped cream into the gooseberry purée. Spoon into 4 small glasses or dishes and chill well. Decorate with elderflowers and serve with sponge fingers or Shortbread Fingers (see page 114).

Cook's Tip
Gooseberry fool can be made without elderflowers. Excellent fruit fools can also be made from strawberries, raspberries, blackberries (which can be puréed raw), blackcurrants, rhubarb and apricots (which need to be cooked first, like the gooseberries). The fruit purée should be the consistency of thick cream. You will need about 150 ml/¼ pint cream for every 450 ml/¾ pint fruit purée.

Thick custard may also be added to a fruit fool to give a more substantial texture.

Preparation time
20–30 minutes, plus chilling time

Serves 4–6

You will need
1 kg/2 lb green gooseberries, topped and tailed
65 ml/2½ fl oz water
2–3 sprigs of elderflowers, plus extra, to decorate
about 175 g/6 oz caster sugar
300 ml/½ pint double cream, whipped until thick and holding its shape

Irish Whiskey Syllabub

Put the lemon rind and juice, honey and whiskey into a large bowl and leave to stand for as long as possible – at least 1 hour – to develop the flavours.

Gradually whisk in the cream until the mixture begins to thicken. Spoon into wine glasses and serve immediately, sprinkled with a little freshly grated nutmeg, or chill until required. Serve with sponge fingers or Shortbread Fingers (see page 114).

Cook's Tips
If the syllabub is left for several hours it will separate into a two-layered delight, with thick cream on top and clear liquid at the bottom.

Syllabub was a popular dessert in the grand houses of Ireland in the eighteenth and nineteenth centuries. This is a truly Irish version, using whiskey, but brandy can be used instead.

Preparation time
15 minutes

Serves 4–6

You will need
grated rind and juice of 1 large lemon
6 tablespoons clear honey
8 tablespoons Irish malt whiskey
300 ml/½ pint double cream, chilled
grated nutmeg

Irish Whiskey Trifle

Cut the Swiss roll into 1 cm/½ inch slices and arrange in a 1.2 litre/2 pint glass bowl. Sprinkle the whiskey over the Swiss roll and top with the raspberries, reserving a few for decoration. Leave to soak while preparing the custard.

For the custard, bring the cream to simmering point. Place the egg yolks, caster sugar and cornflour in a bowl and beat together until pale. Pour on the cream, stirring continually. Return the custard to the saucepan and cook over a low heat, stirring constantly until thick. Leave to cool slightly, then pouring over the trifle and leave to cool completely.

When cold, spread the whipped cream on top of the custard and decorate with the reserved raspberries.

Cook's Tip
This basic trifle can be varied by using a tin of mixed fruit instead of the raspberries; 300 ml/½ pint custard made with custard powder instead of homemade custard; fruit jelly instead of whiskey to moisten the sponge.

Preparation time
30–40 minutes

Serves 6–8

You will need
1 homemade Swiss roll (about 500 g/1 lb), filled with raspberry jam
50 ml/2 fl oz Irish whiskey
250 g/8 oz frozen raspberries
300 ml/½ pint double cream, whipped until thick and holding its shape, to decorate

Custard
300 ml/½ pint double cream
3 egg yolks
25 g/1 oz caster sugar
1 teaspoon cornflour

Apple, Blackberry and Marmalade Crumble

Put the apples into a saucepan with the lemon juice, caster sugar and water and cook gently for 3–5 minutes, until the apples are beginning to soften. Stir in the marmalade and blackberries and pour into a 600–900 ml/1–1½ pint ovenproof pie dish.

For the topping, rub the butter into the flour and stir in the sugar. Scatter over the fruit mixture, pressing it down slightly. Place in a preheated oven at 200°C (400°F), Gas Mark 6 for 20–25 minutes, until the crumble topping is golden.

Cook's Tip
Rhubarb, gooseberries and plums can be used instead of the apples – omit the blackberries with these fruit.

Jumbo or porridge oats can replace some of the flour: use half plain flour and half oats.

Preparation time
30 minutes

Cooking time
20–25 minutes

Oven temperature
200°C (400°F), Gas Mark 6

Serves 4–6

You will need
500 g/1 lb Bramley apples, peeled, cored and sliced
1 tablespoon lemon juice
50–75 g/2–3 oz caster sugar
50 ml/2 fl oz water
2 tablespoons marmalade
125 g/4 oz blackberries, washed

Topping
40 g/1½ oz butter
75 g/3 oz plain flour
40 g/1½ oz demerara sugar

Irish Cheese Plate with Spiced Fruit Compote

Put the red wine, orange juice and water in a large saucepan with the lemon rind and juice. Tie the spices in a piece of muslin and add to the pan. Bring to the boil, add the dried fruit and simmer gently for 30–40 minutes, until the fruit is very tender. Leave until cold.

Cut the cheese into similar-sized wedges and arrange on large individual plates. Spoon a little of the spiced fruit compote on the side, garnish with watercress and serve with oatcakes.

Cook's Tip
Allow approximately 75 g/3 oz of each cheese per person.
The following are some of my favourite Irish cheeses:
Cashel Blue: semi-soft blue
Rathgore: blue-veined goats' cheese, similar to Roquefort
St Tola: goats' cheese, log
Cooleeney: soft Camembert type
Milleens: soft Camembert type
Gubbeens: semi-soft, washed-rind
Gubbeens, smoked: semi-hard
Fivemiletown: oak-smoked
Gabriel: Gruyère type
Desmond: hard, close-textured
Lavistown: semi-hard, Cheshire type
Ring: farmhouse Cheddar type

Preparation time
20 minutes

Cooking time
30–40 minutes

Serves 4

You will need
450 ml/¾ pint red wine
150 ml/¼ pint orange juice
300 ml/½ pint water
grated rind and juice of 1 lemon
5 cm/2 inch stick cinnamon
6 whole peppercorns
6 whole allspice berries
1 blade of mace
375 g/12 oz mixed dried fruit (apricots, peaches, prunes, pears, dates, bananas, figs)

Cheese plate
a selection of 5–8 Irish cheeses (Cook's Tip)
watercress leaves
Irish oatcakes

Irish Apple Tart

Divide the pastry in half and roll out one half to a circle about 4 cm/1½ inches larger than the pie plate. Line the plate with this pastry, trimming off any excess. Arrange the apples on the pastry, sprinkling the layers with the sugar and cloves.

Roll out the remaining pastry to a circle just large enough to cover the tart. Brush the pastry rim with lightly beaten egg white and cover with the pastry lid. Press the edges firmly to seal and flute to decorate. Brush the tart with the remaining egg white and dust with caster sugar.

Place in a preheated oven at 200°C (400°F), Gas Mark 6 for 10 minutes, then reduce the heat to 180°C (350°F), Gas Mark 4 and cook until the pastry is pale golden and the apples are tender when tested with a skewer. Sprinkle with more caster sugar and serve hot or cold, with whipped cream.

Cook's Tip
I like to bake pastry tarts on an enamel plate, as the metal conducts the heat better than glass or china, and ensures that the bottom of the pastry is cooked and crisp.

Preparation time
30 minutes

Cooking time
30–40 minutes

Oven temperature
200°C (400°F), Gas Mark 6, then 180°C (350°F), Gas Mark 4

Serves 6–8

You will need
300g/10 oz Rich Shortcrust Pastry (see page 107)
1.5 kg/3 lb Bramley cooking apples, peeled, cored and thinly sliced
5 tablespoons granulated sugar
6 whole cloves
1 egg white, lightly beaten
caster sugar, to dust

Bakewell Tart

Prepare the pastry following the method on page 107. Roll out two-thirds and use to line a 20 cm/8 inch fluted quiche tin, reserving the remainder. Spread the raspberry jam over the pastry and place the tin on a baking sheet.

For the filling, cream the butter and sugar together until light and fluffy, then gradually add the eggs, ground almonds and flour, beating well after each addition. Stir in the almond essence and pour into the pastry case.

Roll the reserved pastry and trimmings into an 11 x 25 cm/4½ x 10 inch rectangle and cut into 1 cm/½ inch strips. Lay these in a lattice pattern across the top of the tart, pressing the ends into the pastry edge. Place in a preheated oven at 200°C (400°F), Gas Mark 6 for 10–15 minutes, then reduce the heat to 160°C (325°F), Gas Mark 3 and cook for a further 25–30 minutes, until the filling is firm. Serve hot or cold with lightly whipped cream.

Cook's Tip
The filling can also be made using the grated rind and juice of ½ lemon; in this case only 1 egg is needed.

Preparation time
30–40 minutes

Cooking time
25–35 minutes

Oven temperature
200°C (400°F), Gas Mark 6, then 160°C (325°F), Gas Mark 4

Serves 4–6

You will need
175 g/6 oz plain flour
pinch of salt
75 g/3 oz butter or hard margarine
25 g/1 oz hard white fat
1 teaspoon caster sugar
1 egg yolk
2–3 tablespoons cold water
3–4 tablespoons raspberry jam

Filling
125 g/4 oz butter
125 g/4 oz caster sugar
2 eggs (size 2), beaten
125 g/4 oz ground almonds
1 tablespoon plain flour
1 teaspoon almond essence

Brown Bread and Irish Whiskey Ice Cream

Mix together the breadcrumbs and demerara sugar, then spread over a large roasting tray and place in a preheated oven at 240°C (475°F), Gas Mark 9, until the sugar is caramelized; this will take about 10 minutes. Leave until cold.

Whisk the eggs and caster sugar until very thick and pale cream in colour. Fold the caramelized breadcrumbs into the eggs, followed by the whiskey and whipped cream. Pour into a rigid container and freeze overnight.

Serve 2 scoops per person, decorated with a mint leaf and accompanied by Shortbread Fingers (see page 114).

Cook's Tip
Soda bread is not suitable for this ice cream as it makes it rather heavy. Granary bread or any other yeasted brown bread is excellent.

An ice-cream machine is not required: freezing is done in the deep freeze with no stirring or churning necessary.

Preparation time
30 minutes, plus overnight freezing

Cooking time
10 minutes

Oven temperature
240°C (475°F), Gas Mark 9

Serves 9–10

You will need
175 g/6 oz fresh brown breadcrumbs
125 g/4 oz demerara sugar
3 eggs (size 2)
65 g/2½ oz caster sugar
75 ml/3 fl oz Irish whiskey
450 ml/¾ pint double cream, whipped until thick and holding its shape
fresh mint leaves, to decorate

Rich Shortcrust Pastry

Sift the flour and salt into a large mixing bowl. Add the fat and cut into the flour, then rub in with the fingertips until the mixture resembles fine breadcrumbs. Stir in the sugar. Mix the egg yolk with the water and sprinkle over the top of the crumbled mixture. Mix lightly with a broad-bladed knife until a stiff dough forms. Work only long enough for the mixture to form a ball, then wrap and leave to rest in the refrigerator for about 30 minutes before using.

Cook's Tips
The food processor is a most convenient way to make shortcrust pastry and gives excellent results. Success, however, depends on careful processing to ensure that the dough is not overworked.

Pastry freezes well; defrost for several hours or overnight in the refrigerator.

To make a double-crust 20 cm/8 inch tart, or 8 x 11 cm/4½ inch tartlets, you will need 250 g/8 oz pastry: double the quantities, but use only 1 egg yolk and 3–4 tablespoons cold water.

To make a double-crust 25 cm/10 inch tart, you will need 300 g/10 oz plain flour, 150 g/5 oz butter and 75 g/3 oz white fat. Use 1 tablespoon caster sugar and mix the egg yolk with 4–5 tablespoons cold water.

Preparation time
15 minutes

Makes 1 x 20 cm/ 8 inch tart

You will need
125 g/4 oz plain flour
pinch of salt
50 g/2 oz butter or hard margarine
25 g/1 oz hard white fat
1 teaspoon caster sugar
1 egg yolk
2 tablespoons cold water

Steamed Apple Sponge Pudding

Put the apples in a saucepan with half the butter and 1 tablespoon water and cook gently until soft. Stir in the sugar. Use the remaining butter to grease a 1.2 litre/2 pint pudding basin or 6 x 175 ml/6 fl oz moulds. Put the stewed apples into the bottom.

To make the sponge, cream the butter and sugar together until light and fluffy, then gradually add the eggs and yolk, beating well after each addition. Fold in the flour, milk, lemon rind and juice. Spoon the sponge mixture over the apples to come three-quarters of the way up the sides of the basin or moulds. Cover with buttered foil and place in a steamer or large saucepan half-full of hot water. Steam or boil the individual puddings for 20–30 minutes, the large for 1–1 ½ hours, topping up the pan with boiling water if necessary.

Turn the cooked pudding(s) on to a plate or plates and serve hot with extra stewed apples, fresh cream or custard.

Cook's Tip
Stewed plums, rhubarb, gooseberries or cherries could be used instead of the apples or replace the fruit with 2–3 tablespoons golden syrup, raspberry or strawberry jam. 125 g/4 oz dried fruit, chopped cherries or dates could be added to the sponge before folding in the flour.

Preparation time
20 minutes

Cooking time
Individual puddings 40 minutes; large pudding 1–1½ hours

Serves 6

You will need
375 g/12 oz Bramley apples, peeled, cored and sliced
25 g/1 oz butter
125 g/4 oz caster sugar

Sponge
125 g/4 oz butter
150 g/5 oz caster sugar
2 eggs (size 2)
1 egg yolk
200 g/7 oz self-raising flour
2 tablespoons milk
finely grated rind and juice of ½ lemon

Treacle Tart

Roll the pastry thinly and use to line a 20 cm/8 inch fluted loose-bottomed quiche tin about 4 cm/1½ inches deep.

Mix together the ingredients for the filling and pour into the pastry case. Place in a preheated oven at 190°C (375°F), Gas Mark 5 for 20–30 minutes, until the pastry is cooked and golden. Serve hot or cold with lightly whipped cream.

Cook's Tip
The tart can also be latticed with strips of pastry as in Bakewell Tart, in which case you will need 175 g/6 oz of pastry (see page 104).

Preparation time
20–30 minutes

Cooking time
20–30 minutes

Oven temperature
190°C (375°F), Gas Mark 5

Serves 6–8

You will need
125 g/4 oz Rich Shortcrust Pastry (see page 107)

Filling
175 g/6 oz fresh white breadcrumbs
325 g/11 oz golden syrup
grated rind and juice (approximately 50 ml/2 fl oz) of 1 lemon

St Brendan's Cream

Mix the liqueur, wine, lemon juice and sugar in a bowl and whisk with an electric beater to dissolve the sugar. Gradually add the cream, whisking all the time until the liquid begins to thicken. The mixture will look slightly curdled at first but will improve in texture as the whisking continues. When the mixture holds its shape, spoon into long-stemmed glasses. Chill for several hours before serving to develop the flavours. Decorate with lemon slices.

Cook's Tip
This is one of the new Irish desserts created to use a popular cream liqueur The recipe is based on the medieval syllabub but is less solid in texture.

Preparation time
15 minutes, plus chilling time

Serves 6

You will need
125 ml/4 fl oz St Brendan's or Bailey's Irish Cream liqueur
50 ml/2 fl oz sweet white wine
2 tablespoons lemon juice
50 g/2 oz caster sugar
300 ml/½ pint double cream
thin slices of lemon, to decorate

Bramley Apple Cheesecake

Melt the butter in a small saucepan, add the biscuit crumbs and mix well. Press into the bottom of a lightly oiled 20 cm/ 8 inch loose-bottomed cake tin about 5 cm/2 inches deep.

For the filling, put the apples in a saucepan with the lemon juice and 1 tablespoon water and cook gently until soft. Stir in the sugar and egg yolks and leave until cold.

Add the cheese to the cooked apples and blend in a liquidizer or food processor until smooth. Pour into a large bowl.

Dissolve the gelatine in 3 tablespoons water and add to the apple mixture. Lightly whisk the egg whites and fold into the mixture along with the cream. Pour into the tin and refrigerate until set; this will take at least 4 hours, or overnight.

Remove the cheesecake from the tin and decorate with rosettes of cream and apple slices.

Cook's Tip
Soaking the apple slices for the decoration in a little lemon juice prevents them from discolouring.

Preparation time
30 minutes, plus setting time

Serves 8–10

You will need
50 g/2 oz unsalted butter
150 g/5 oz digestive biscuits, crushed

Filling
1 kg/2 lb Bramley apples, peeled, cored and sliced
1 tablespoon lemon juice
75 g/3 oz caster sugar
2 eggs (size 2), separated
250 g/8 oz cream cheese or ricotta cheese
15 g/½ oz powdered gelatine
250 ml/8 fl oz double cream, lightly whipped

To decorate
150 ml/¼ pint double cream
thin slices of red-skinned apple

Irish Coffee

Warm a stemmed whiskey glass or Paris goblet with hot water; discard the water. Put the sugar in the bottom of the glass and add very hot coffee to come to within 5 cm/ 2 inches of the top of the glass. Stir to dissolve the sugar, then add the whiskey.

Hold a teaspoon, curved side upwards, across the glass, barely touching the coffee and pour the cream very slowly over the spoon so that it floats on top of the coffee. The cream should be suspended on top of the whiskey-laced coffee (it hasn't worked if it falls to the bottom). The coffee is drunk through the cold cream.

Cook's Tip
For health and long life drink daily!

Preparation time
5 minutes

Serves 1

You will need
1 heaped teaspoon demerara sugar
strong black coffee
1 double measure (½ gill, or 65 ml/ 2½ fl oz) of Irish whiskey
1–2 tablespoons chilled double cream

Of all the traditions in Irish cookery, baking is one of the strongest. Buttermilk breads such as white and brown soda, scones and pancakes are served at all times of the day in homes throughout the country, and with a profusion of other baked products the Irish table is seldom empty.

Breads, Cakes and Baking

Shortbread Fingers

Cream the butter and sugar together until light and fluffy. Sift in the flour and cornflour and mix well to combine. Press into a 30 x 20 cm/12 x 8 inch baking tin and mark the surface with the prongs of a fork. Place in a preheated oven at 140°C (275°F), Gas Mark 1 for 30 minutes, then reduce the heat to 120°C (250°F), Gas Mark ½ and cook for a further 1–1½ hours, until golden brown.

Remove the shortbread from the oven and cut into fingers. Sprinkle with caster sugar and leave to cool slightly in the tin, then transfer to a wire rack until cold. Store in an airtight tin.

Cook's Tip
For a crunchier texture, replace 25 g/1 oz of the flour with 25 g/1 oz semolina.

Preparation time
15 minutes

Cooking time
1½–2 hours

Oven temperature
140°C (275°F), Gas Mark 1, then 120°C (250°F), Gas Mark ½

Makes 32–36 biscuits

You will need
250 g/8 oz butter
125 g/4 oz caster sugar
300 g/10 oz plain flour
50 g/2 oz cornflour
caster sugar, for dusting

White Soda Bread

Sift the flour, bicarbonate of soda and salt into a large mixing bowl; add sugar to sweeten. Make a well in the centre and pour in 400 ml/14 fl oz of the buttermilk, mixing lightly with a broad-bladed knife or wooden spoon to form a spongy dough, adding more buttermilk if necessary.

Use the butter to grease a 19 x 11 cm/7½ x 4½ inch loaf tin and turn the porridge-like dough into the tin, spreading it into the corners but leaving the surface rough. Sprinkle with a little flour, place on a baking sheet and bake in a preheated oven at 200°C (400°F), Gas Mark 6 for 30 minutes. Reduce the heat to 150°C (300°F), Gas Mark 2 and cook for a further 30 minutes, until the bread is well risen, pale beige and crusty on top.

Remove from the oven and cover with a clean cloth. After 5 minutes, turn out of the tin, wrap in the cloth and leave to cool before cutting. Serve sliced, with butter.

Cook's Tips
If soda bread flour is not available, use plain flour with 1 heaped teaspoon bicarbonate of soda and 1 heaped teaspoon cream of tartar.

The secret of good soda bread is to mix quickly and lightly and not to overwork. Use just enough buttermilk to form a dough.

Preparation time
10 minutes

Cooking time
1 hour

Oven temperature
200°C (400°F), Gas Mark 6, then 150°C (300°F), Gas Mark 2

Makes 1 x 1 kg/ 2 lb loaf

You will need
500 g/1 lb soda bread flour
1 teaspoon bicarbonate of soda
1 teaspoon salt
25–50 g/1–2 oz caster sugar
400–475 ml/14–16 fl oz buttermilk
25 g/1 oz butter

Dropped Scones (Pancakes)

Sift the flour into a large mixing bowl, stir in the sugar and make a well in the centre. Break in the egg and beat with a wooden spoon to make a thick, smooth batter, gradually adding the buttermilk and drawing the flour from the sides of the bowl to the centre.

Heat a griddle or heavy cast-iron frying pan over a gentle heat. Grease lightly with a knob of butter, wiping most of it off with kitchen paper. Drop tablespoons of the batter on to the pan. The scones will immediately begin to rise. When a few bubbles begin to break on the surface, gently flip the scones over and brown on the second side. When the scones are cooked they should be golden brown and spongy in texture.

Wrap in a clean cloth and keep warm until all the scones are cooked. Serve warm, with butter and jam.

Cook's Tip
If soda bread flour is not available, use 125 g/4 oz plain flour with 1 teaspoon bicarbonate of soda and 1 teaspoon cream of tartar.

Preparation time
5 minutes

Cooking time
15 minutes

Makes 14 small pancakes

You will need
125 g/4 oz soda bread flour
25 g/1 oz caster sugar
1 egg (size 2)
150 ml/¼ pint buttermilk
butter for cooking

Irish Wheaten Bread (Brown Soda)

Sift the soda bread flour and bicarbonate of soda into a large mixing bowl, add the wholemeal flour, salt and sugar, stirring to blend. Make a well in the centre and pour in 400 ml/14 fl oz of the buttermilk, stirring with a broad-bladed knife or wooden spoon to form a loose dough, adding more milk if necessary.

Use the butter to grease a 19 x 11 cm/7½ x 4 ½ inch loaf tin. Turn the dough into the tin, leaving the surface rough. Sprinkle with a little extra wholemeal flour to give a nutty surface. Place on a baking sheet and bake in a preheated oven at 200°C (400°F), Gas Mark 6 for 30 minutes. Reduce the heat to 150°C (300°F), Gas Mark 2 and cook for a further 30 minutes, until the bread is well risen, brown, crusty on top and when a skewer inserted into the centre comes out clean.

Remove from the oven, turn out, wrap in a clean cloth and leave on a wire rack until cold. Serve sliced, with butter.

Cook's Tips
Traditionally, good-sized breakfast cups would be used for measuring: 1 cup plain or soda bread flour to 2 cups wholemeal flour and 1 cup buttermilk.

.All 'soda'-style breads need to be eaten the day they are baked or toasted or fried the following day.

Preparation time
10 minutes

Cooking time
1 hour

Oven temperature
200°C (400°F), Gas Mark 6, then 150°C (300°F), Gas Mark 2

Makes 1 x 1 kg/ 2 lb loaf

You will need
175 g/6 oz soda bread flour
1 teaspoon bicarbonate of soda
375 g/12 oz wholemeal flour
pinch of salt
1–2 teaspoons brown sugar
400–475 ml/14–16 fl oz buttermilk
15 g/½ oz butter

Currant Soda

Sift the flour and bicarbonate of soda into a large mixing bowl, then stir in the salt, sugar and fruit. Make a well in the centre and pour in 400 ml/14 fl oz of the buttermilk. Mix lightly with a broad-bladed knife or wooden spoon to form a loose dough, adding the rest of the buttermilk if necessary.

Use the butter to grease a 20 cm/8 inch round deep cake tin. Turn the dough into the tin, leaving the surface rough. Sprinkle with a little flour, place on a baking sheet and bake in a preheated oven at 200°C (400°F), Gas Mark 6 for 30 minutes. Reduce the heat to 150°C (300°F), Gas Mark 2 and cook for a further 30 minutes, until the bread is golden brown and crisp to the touch. A skewer inserted into the centre should come out clean.

Remove from the oven, turn out, wrap in a clean cloth and leave on a wire rack until cold. Serve sliced, with butter.

Cook's Tip
Savoury soda bread can be made by replacing the dried fruit with a mixture of cooked, chopped bacon or ham, chopped herbs and grated, strongly flavoured Cheddar-type cheese.

Preparation time
10–15 minutes

Cooking time
1–1¼ hours

Oven temperature
200°C (400°F), Gas Mark 6, then 150°C (300°F), Gas Mark 2

Makes 1 x 20 cm/ 8 inch round loaf

You will need
500 g/1 lb soda bread flour
1 heaped teaspoon bicarbonate of soda
pinch of salt
50 g/2 oz caster sugar
125 g/4 oz dried fruit
400–475 ml/14–16 fl oz buttermilk
15 g/½ oz butter

Buttermilk Scones

Sift the dry ingredients into a bowl. Cut the butter into small pieces and rub into the flour until the mixture resembles fine breadcrumbs. Make a well in the centre and add almost all the buttermilk, mixing lightly with a broad-bladed knife to form a soft dough.

Turn on to a lightly floured work surface and knead very gently to form a ball. Roll out to about 2 cm/¾ inch thick. Cut into scones, using a 5–6 cm/2–2½ inch cutter.

Place on a lightly floured baking sheet and brush with egg or milk to glaze. Place in a preheated oven at 220°C (425°F), Gas Mark 7 for 15–20 minutes, until well risen and light golden. Serve hot or cold with butter or jam.

Cook's Tips
For wheaten scones use half wholemeal and half plain flour.

For fruit scones, add 25–50 g/1–2 oz dried fruit or cherries and 25–50 g/1–2 oz caster sugar before adding the milk.

For savoury scones, add 50 g/2 oz grated cheese, some chopped herbs, and diced cooked bacon, if liked.

Preparation time
15 minutes

Cooking time
15–20 minutes

Oven temperature
220°C (425°F),Gas Mark 7

Makes 8–12 scones

You will need
250 g/8 oz plain flour
1 teaspoon bicarbonate of soda
1 teaspoon cream of tartar
pinch of salt
25 g/1 oz butter
200 ml/7 fl oz buttermilk
beaten egg or milk, to glaze (optional)

Tea Brack

Put the fruit and sugar into a large bowl and pour on the hot tea. Stir to dissolve the sugar and leave overnight to allow the fruit to swell.

Line the base and sides of a 20 cm/8 inch round deep cake tin with greaseproof paper and grease lightly but evenly with the melted butter.

Sift the flour, baking powder and spice together and mix into the fruit mixture alternately with the eggs, beating well after each addition. Pour into the prepared tin, smooth the top and place in a preheated oven at 160°C (325°F), Gas Mark 3 for approximately 1½ hours, until a skewer inserted into the centre comes out clean.

Leave to cool in the tin, then turn on to a wire rack.
When cold, store in an airtight tin.

Preparation time
15 minutes, plus overnight soaking

Cooking time
1½ hours

Oven temperature
160°C (325°F), Gas Mark 3

Makes 1 x 20 cm/ 8 inch round cake

You will need
275 g/9 oz sultanas
275 g/9 oz raisins
250 g/8 oz soft dark brown sugar
475 ml/16 fl oz strong black hot tea
15 g/½ oz butter, melted
375 g/12 oz plain flour
2 teaspoons baking powder
2 teaspoons mixed spice
2 eggs (size 2), beaten

Chocolate Cake with Whiskey Cream

Line the base and sides of a 20 cm/8 inch round deep cake tin with greaseproof paper. Lightly oil and dust with a mixture of 1 tablespoon flour and 1 tablespoon caster sugar.

Beat the eggs with the sugar until thick and pale. Sift the flour with the cocoa powder. Fold gently into the egg mixture one-third at a time, adding the water with the last third. Pour into the prepared tin and bake in a preheated oven at 190°C (375°F), Gas Mark 5 for 25–30 minutes. Leave to cool slightly in the tin, then turn on to a wire rack to cool completely.

When cold, slice the cake into 3 layers. Place 1 layer on a serving plate, spread with some apricot jam, sprinkle with half the whiskey and cover with half the cream. Cover with another layer of sponge and the remaining filling. Top with the last layer of sponge and finish with a dusting of icing sugar or chocolate topping (Cook's Tip). Decorate with rosettes of whipped cream and garnish with chocolate.

Cook's Tip
To make a chocolate topping, break 250 g/8 oz dark chocolate into a bowl over a pan of hot water, add 1 tablespoon whiskey and 15 g/½ oz butter and stir until the chocolate has melted. Add 1 beaten egg and 1 tablespoon double cream.

Preparation time
30 minutes

Cooking time
25–30 minutes

Oven temperature
190°C (375°F), Gas Mark 5

Makes 1 x 20 cm/ 8 inch round cake

You will need
3 eggs
125 g/4 oz caster sugar
75 g/3 oz self-raising flour
50 g/2 oz cocoa powder
2 tablespoons warm water

Filling
3 tablespoons apricot jam
2 tablespoons whiskey
300 ml/½ pint double cream, lightly whipped

To decorate
icing sugar or chocolate topping (Cook's Tip)
150 ml/¼ pint double cream, whipped until stiff
chocolate flakes, leaves or grated chocolate

Soda Farls

Sift the flour and salt into a bowl. Make a well in the centre and add 250 ml/8 fl oz of the buttermilk. Mix lightly with a broad-bladed knife to form a firm dough, adding the remaining buttermilk if necessary.

Turn on to a lightly floured surface and knead lightly until a smooth ball is formed. Roll or pat out to form a circle approximately 20 cm/8 inches in diameter and no more than 1 cm/½ inch thick. Cut into quarters to make 4 farls.

Heat a griddle or heavy cast-iron frying pan over a gentle heat, sprinkle with flour and when this turns pale beige, the temperature is correct for cooking. Place the farls on the pan and cook for 6–10 minutes on each side, until risen and pale beige. When cooked, they will sound hollow when tapped.

Remove from the pan, wrap in a clean cloth and leave to cool slightly. Serve warm, sliced in half and generously buttered.

Cook's Tips
If soda bread flour is not available, use plain flour with ½ teaspoon bicarbonate of soda and ½ teaspoon cream of tartar.

Soda farls are an important feature of an Ulster Fry (see page 64) and as the container for a fried egg, bacon and sausage for a quick snack known as a sausage soda.

Preparation time
10–15 minutes

Cooking time
12–20 minutes

Makes 4 farls

You will need
300 g/10 oz soda bread flour, plus extra, for dusting
1 teaspoon salt
250–300 ml/8–10 fl oz buttermilk

Boiled Fruit Cake

Line the base and sides of an 18 cm/7 inch round deep cake tin with greaseproof paper and grease well with butter.

Put the butter, sugar, fruit and water into a large saucepan, bring to the boil, then simmer for 10 minutes. Leave to cool.

Sift the flour, raising agents and spice together and fold into the fruit mixture, along with the almond essence and beaten eggs. Pour into the prepared tin and place in a preheated oven at 150°C (300°F), Gas Mark 2 for 1½ hours, until risen and firm, and a skewer inserted into the centre comes out clean.

Leave to cool in the tin, then turn on to a wire rack to cool completely. Wrap in greaseproof paper or foil and store in an airtight tin. Serve sliced, with butter if liked.

Preparation time
20–30 minutes

Cooking time
1½ hours

Oven temperature
150°C (300°F), Gas Mark 2

Makes 1 x 18 cm/ 7 inch round cake

You will need
150 g/5 oz butter
150 g/5 oz soft brown sugar
375 g/12 oz dried mixed fruit
250 ml/8 fl oz water
250 g/8 oz plain flour
1 teaspoon baking powder
1 teaspoon bicarbonate of soda
2 teaspoons mixed spice
½ teaspoon almond essence
2 eggs, beaten

Raspberry and Cream Sponge

Grease 2 x 15 cm/6 inch sandwich tins and dust with a mixture of flour and caster sugar.

Put the eggs and sugar in a large bowl, stand this over a pan of hot water and whisk until light and creamy. Alternatively, use an electric mixer. The mixture should be stiff enough to retain the impression of the whisk for a few seconds; this will take about 5–8 minutes. Remove from the heat and continue whisking until cold.

Sift the flour and baking powder together and very lightly fold into the whisked mixture, one-third at a time. Divide the mixture between the prepared tins and bake near the top of a preheated oven at 180°C (350°F), Gas Mark 4, for 20 minutes. Leave in the tins until cold, then turn out.

Sandwich the cakes together with the jam and cream and dust with sieved icing sugar.

Cook's Tip
For a larger cake, use 2 x 20 cm/8 inch tins and 4 eggs (size 2); cook for an extra 15 minutes.

Preparation time
15 minutes

Cooking time
20 minutes

Oven temperature
180°C (350°F), Gas Mark 4

Makes 1 x 15 cm/ 6 inch round cake

You will need
3 eggs
125 g/4 oz caster sugar
75 g/3 oz plain flour
¼ teaspoon baking powder
3–4 tablespoons raspberry jam
150 ml/¼ pint double cream, whipped until stiff
icing sugar, for dusting

Irish Oatcakes

Put the oatmeal into a large bowl. Sift the flour, bicarbonate of soda, cream of tartar and salt on top and make a well in the centre. Put the butter and water into a small saucepan and bring to the boil. Pour into the well and mix to bind.

Turn on to a work surface lightly sprinkled with oatmeal and roll out the dough to form a cake about 23 cm/9 inches in diameter and 3 mm/⅛ inch thick. Sprinkle more oatmeal on top of the cake and press it into the surface. Cut into 8 triangles. Arrange the triangles on a lightly floured baking sheet and place in a preheated oven at 180°C (350°F), Gas Mark 4 for about 40 minutes.

Preparation time
15 minutes

Cooking time
40 minutes

Oven temperature
180°C (350°F), Gas Mark 4

Makes 8 oatcakes

You will need
250 g/8 oz medium or fine oatmeal, plus extra for shaping
50 g/2 oz plain flour
½ teaspoon bicarbonate of soda
¼ teaspoon cream of tartar
½ teaspoon salt
50 g/2 oz butter
50 ml/2 fl oz hot water

Potato Apple Cake

Put the mashed potatoes into a large bowl and mix in the salt and 25 g/1 oz of the butter. Stir in the flour to make a pliable dough. Turn on to a lightly floured surface and divide the dough in half. Roll out each piece to form a 20 cm/8 inch circle. Divide the sliced apples between the circles, piling them on one half only. Moisten the edge of the circles with a little water and fold the uncovered half of the potato bread over the apples to form a half-moon shape. Press the edges together to seal.

Heat a griddle or heavy cast-iron frying pan over a gentle heat. Cook the cakes for 15–20 minutes on each side to cook the apples and brown the bread.

Remove the cakes from the pan and place on a serving plate. Carefully open the cakes along the curved edges, fold back the dough, sprinkle the apples with sugar and dot with the remaining butter. Re-seal the edges and put the cakes in a preheated oven at 200°C (400°F), Gas Mark 5 for 5–10 minutes to form a thick syrup. Serve hot.

Cook's Tip
The potato apple can also be eaten cold, in which case a little sugar should be added to the apples before cooking and the outside of the cake buttered before serving.

Preparation time
15 minutes

Cooking time
45–50 minutes

Oven temperature
200°C (400°F), Gas Mark 6

Makes 2 large cakes

You will need
250 g/8 oz warm potatoes, cooked and mashed
½ teaspoon salt
75 g/3 oz butter
50 g/2 oz plain flour
300 g/10 oz Bramley apples, peeled, cored and very thinly sliced
caster sugar, to sweeten

Index